LIKE SOCKS ON A ROOSTER

MIKE FICARA

Published by:

The Ghost Publishing, USA

Paperback ISBN-13: 978 -1-7371531-9-1

Ebook ISBN-13: 978 1-7372350-0-2

DEDICATION

This book is dedicated to my wife, Lauren Ficara. Without her love and support, I could have never gone on this journey.

FOREWORD

In a world of online entrepreneurship and influencers with an MBA in social media, it's easy to think that you can build a highly profitable and sustainable business just by posting a picture on Instagram.

And while posting on Instagram (or any social media outlet) is certainly valuable to growing your business and brand, Mike and I both have real-world experience in building businesses going back to before the online thing totally exploded. The value of this is that we have hands-on knowledge of the back-end operations and the real-world nuts and bolts that are actually required for scale and impact.

Which, I assume, is what everyone in business is trying to achieve, right?

You see, building a successful business sustainably is more than just front-end optics. Yes, getting noticed and making your first few sales is really important, but the reason most people struggle to scale is not because they don't know how to look good online but because they don't understand the back-end strategies that make the front-end successes possible.

There is also a misunderstanding of the foundational aspects that really make it possible to not only build a business but keep it growing year after year.

And that is exactly what Mike brings to you in such a clear and digestible way, here in this book. The essentials that hardly anyone talks about and even fewer people ever truly master.

When Mike and I met back in 2018, we were both in a place of rapid growth and transition. I had just left the world of small business management the year before and was hustling to grow my personal brand and coaching business, as Mike was scaling his own brand and consulting company, The MAGS Group.

At the time, I was hosting a weekly *live* show on Facebook called Real Talk in Real Time, where I brought on guests who were thriving in the space of entrepreneurship.

Every week, we would jam about the reality of what it takes to be successful as an entrepreneur. And in showing up consistently like that, I was able to attract clients and it became the primary way that I built my coaching business during my initial year and half.

I don't remember the exact message that got our conversation started, but I remember that it all started with a Direct Message on Facebook, and that, at that time, I was persistent in building connections and networking with people I met online and so was he.

That Direct Message thread led to our first phone call where he mentioned that he appreciated that I was shedding light on the truth of what it means to really be an entrepreneur, and we immediately clicked on that point.

I asked him what was challenging him the most in his business (at that time). He responded with an all-too-common answer: he wasn't sure how to talk to people about what he does, which led to a struggle in closing more clients because it can be hard to close someone when you aren't even really sure how to start the conversation. It's even harder when you start the conversation but don't know how to move the conversation into the close.

We shared a laugh together because that is often one of the hardest parts about establishing yourself in the world of business: effectively communicating to others how you can help them, clearly expressing what you do in a way that isn't mundane or obscure, then guiding them toward a service that you know can help them solve their pain, and then closing the deal.

Let me tell you, I have coached new entrepreneurs and vetted business pros alike, and you would be surprised to learn how many of them totally miss the mark on this and *never* invest the time or money to get the help to figure those things out.

I'm sharing this part of our backstory because Mike is going to touch on these very concepts of consistency, networking, and scalability throughout this book, which is to say that everything he talks about in this book does, in fact, *work*. Our relationship is proof of that. And that's exactly how he went from being a total stranger on Facebook to becoming a coaching client of mine to eventually becoming one of my greatest friends to date.

Mike and I both come from non-traditional business backgrounds that afforded us a diversity in experience and perspective and what I believe to be a more realistic and grounded understanding of what being in business is about—and what it takes to succeed.

After that initial conversation, I had the pleasure of coaching Mike for a little over a year, and every day after that, I watched Mike take everything he was learning in every aspect of his business and apply it with commitment and conviction.

He can write this book for you today because he has spent the last 10 years, if not more, figuring these very things out himself. Now he's helping other entrepreneurs like you to build their multi-million-dollar brands by applying the same principles he's sharing here in this book.

And as they say, the proof is always in the pudding!

Which is why I believe Mike wrote this book—to remind people not only why the basics matter (and how they affect your bottom line), but that everyone in business needs to have this stuff figured out if they're going to succeed; not just for now but over the long term.

Over the years, Mike and I have enjoyed many conversations about the myths of entrepreneurship and all the misguided things we see in the online or "influencer" space. From people sharing their "get rich quick" strategies and their "fake it 'til you make it" mantras, and the many other things that really don't do justice to the real experiences and the often-harsh realities faced by most people who are trying to work their way to the top.

I think Mike and I both have this sort of "no bullshit" perspective because both of us were raised by *true* entrepreneur parents who earned their stripes in the world of business before the Internet, influencers, and Instagram were a thing.

Having our parents as real-life examples, we grew up with an understanding of what hard-earned success looks like, and as a result of following in their footsteps, we came to learn our own lessons about how to do this whole "entrepreneur thing" right.

Which is exactly what *Like Socks On A Rooster* is about and why, when it comes to the world of business, this is the perfect book for the times we're in right now.

Many gurus out there spend more time talking about *their own* success than they do speaking to the truth of what it *really* takes to build a successful business. There's a lot of noise out there, and with even more people screaming from the rooftops about how they've done it, it's becoming increasingly more difficult to know who to trust or whose advice to listen to.

Many of these influencer types have success but aren't keeping it *real* with you about what it actually takes. Most of them are more concerned with looking successful than they are with teaching you what actually creates lasting success.

They're just showing you the highs, the flashy cars, the mansions… anything, really, that looks good on the news feed.

Others are totally bullshitting you with hype and cheap tricks to make money fast but not sustainably, while they themselves are still in the rat race of trying to "make it."

Both camps are missing the practical, solid, foundational aspects that can serve as the core for any entrepreneur in business. The basics that can help anyone get going and stay going over the long term.

Which is why I think so many people never get very far in business. Because they never get the full picture of what they should really be focusing their time, attention, and energy on. And as a result, so many people are trying to jump through hoops trying to do *all the things,* instead of focusing on all the *right* things.

Like Bruce Lee famously said, "I fear not the man who has practiced 10,000 kicks once, but I do fear the man who has practiced one kick 10,000 times." And that is what mastery is all about. That is where the secret of success in business lies. In practicing the right things ten-thousand times, so that you can become a master in those things, and so your business can thrive.

Which is exactly what this book creates clarity on. It provides you with the essentials that you need to thrive in your business in a way that is straightforward and isn't overly complicated, written in a way that is guaranteed to make you smile along the way and embrace the challenges of building a business with a much-needed sense of humor.

For those of you who haven't yet hired someone to coach you in gaining clarity on those things, or even if you have, *Like Socks On a Rooster* is here to help you get out of your own way and lay the proper foundation you need to do it right.

This book provides a practical roadmap for any entrepreneur with the essentials you need to build yourself a strong foundation in your business. And I can't think of a more perfect person to have written this book, because nothing is truer to his character and to the power of the work that he does in the world.

Mike doesn't just serve from his heart, he really is passionate about seeing other people succeed. And that's why he is the best person to write this book for you, because while other people are out there showing off how successful *they* are, Mike is here to help *you* become more successful, yourself.

Which is why I believe he wrote this book. Because he actually cares about your success and wants to see more people out in the world doing what they love *more* successfully. There is no one else I trust more than Mike to guide you in both confronting the myths that heavily cloud the entrepreneurial space and the practical knowledge to succeed beyond those myths.

And if that's what you're interested in learning, then you're in the right place and in really good hands.

Natalia Diane

Business Strategist and Co-Founder of 6 Figure Seminars

INTRODUCTION

I love helping those with an entrepreneurial spirit. Those courageous people who have the drive and desire to be successful, most often need a roadmap on how to get there. With so many false and flat-out erroneous methodologies, philosophies, and "best practices" out there, many more entrepreneurs fail than succeed.

At my core, I'm an educator. I started as a substitute teacher and fell in love with education. I grew in my career and eventually became an administrator. My career track would have led me to the principal's chair one day if I hadn't accidentally started to work for a startup. Today, I'm still an educator, but now I educate business owners, teaching them how to traverse the murky waters of building, growing, and scaling their businesses. For business owners, it's usually not all about making money; for most, they have a passion to impact and help others. I've found that those who have that generosity mindset have been able to overcome adversity better than those who solely focus on making a profit. That's the reason why I say, "You have to put passion before profits."

Part of why I love what I do is because I love to allow my creativity to take over. I enjoy working on my podcasts, making videos, Facebook Lives, and other things that allow my personality to shine while educating and inspiring others. In fact, at the beginning of many of my videos, I dance! By no means would I be considered for Dancing with the Stars, So You Think You Can Dance, or Jennifer Lopez's World of Dance, because the fact is, I'm not a dancer—at all. I do it to engage with others in a transparent and fun way.

When people see me dance, they resonate with me because I'm not trying to impress them by my dance moves; I'm just having fun. By not taking myself overly seriously in the beginning, it puts people at ease; subconsciously, they give me a level of trust that a 30-minute speech couldn't produce. That's part of the power of creating a personal brand.

By sharing my ideologies, strategies and humor through videos, I don't believe there's any way I can lose. The worst-case scenario would be that no one watches them, but even then I will have left my children and grandkids a story that they can binge-watch about how their freethinking great-grandfather grew a business through social media.

So many people are caught up today in building generational wealth. This isn't a bad goal, but what if you could create that wealth while you leave behind a wealth of content that can be emulated for decades to come? My story is told online. Maybe my kids won't watch it, but my future grandkids, great grandkids, or someone I may never meet might.

I met one particular entrepreneur at an educational convention. These are usually large events, but this was a small one for Florida charter schools held in Orlando. I was there to assist a client I was working with at the time. After lunch, I passed a booth with a sign that read, Top Score Writing, and this is where I met Lisa Collum for the first time. She happened to have a table where she was selling her writing program. Among all the book and educational technology companies with their fancy set ups, Lisa's 3-ring binders and simple setup caught my eye; she struck me as someone who was a go-getter, but also as someone who could possibly use help in growing her brand and business. I spoke with her and was enthralled by her story.

"When I started teaching writing classes, there wasn't a curriculum, so I created one. The results amazed me and my students! Prior to when I got there, 80-90% of the students had failing test scores. Once I started teaching my system of writing, the scores flipped to where 80-90% of the students passed!"

The passion in her face and the excitement in her voice were compelling. This is the type of person I've been called to help, I thought to myself. However, as her business was still in the infancy stage and she was still doing it on the side, we weren't quite ready for each other. I kept tabs on her, and two years after we met, I told her that I could turn her binders into a digital product. She saw the vision right away and we began working together. Once we completed the online product she asked me, "Okay, now... how do I sell this?"

She had built a very respectable business without any sales and marketing experience, without any training on how to establish systems that would help her grow from a solo-preneur to a legitimate business. I continued to work with her and within eighteen months her low six-figure-a-year business turned into a million-dollar business. Lisa and I still work together, and we continue to grow her now multi-million dollar business year after year.

Today, Lisa Collum has been on television shows, she's an author, and not only has her company, Top Score Writing, gone from one school in one county to serve many schools in various states and multiple counties, she has also bought—and continues to run—her own charter school!

Lisa is not the only business owner I've helped crash through the perpetual ceiling. I've sat in boardrooms across the United States, Central America, and the Middle East, meeting with wildly successful entrepreneurs, business owners, and high-level executives. I've been in strategic sessions and partnered with some incredibly innovative people. I've taught hundreds of entrepreneurs how to figure out their next steps and the importance of working smarter not harder through the implementation of the right systems and processes.

I know what it's like to go all-in. I've bet on myself by putting my house, my family, my marriage, and my future all on the line. But the risk has been worth the reward to the point that, as of the writing of this book, I am married to an amazing woman, we have four kids, I'm getting a swimming pool installed in our forever home, and I'm driving my dream car. I've been down many roads. I've tasted success, and I know how quickly it can come and how quickly it can go. Many people are comfortable remaining at their status quo and not leaving their comfort zone. I live, work, and play outside of the comfort zone, evidenced by my silly dancing when I start my videos.

I wrote this book for many reasons. One is for that kid who is the eighteen-year-old version of me. He or she just got out of high school and isn't sure what they want to do. They've been told that the road to success hinges on going to a good college, getting a degree, and working their way up the corporate ladder. I want to tell those kids—there's another way.

I wrote this book for the millions of entrepreneurs today. Forbes.com states that more than 80% of businesses fail in the first five years. I hope this book finds them before it's too late. This book is designed to demystify the dumb clichés of business ownership and replace them with solid, proven methodologies and tactics that I've personally used to help people like Lisa Collum grow their businesses.

Ultimately, this book will provide clarity for business owners as to what's important and what isn't. Applying the specific strategies and methods I teach here will allow them to obtain their own version of success.

Whether you're that kid right out of school or a sixty-year-old entrepreneur or somewhere in between, I want to tell you that you're not alone. Turn the page and let me help.

TABLE OF CONTENTS

CHAPTER 1

CONGRATULATIONS, YOU DID IT! WORLD'S BEST CUP OF COFFEE

Congratulations Are in Order

Congratulations on starting your own business. You are among the estimated 14% of the population with the courage to strike out on your own. At some point, you decided to leave a job that most likely paid you fairly well and even gave you and your family some type of health insurance. But even with all that stability, your determination to be your own boss, to captain your own ship, to create your own path to financial wellness and respectability compelled you to start your business.

Seriously, congratulations on being brave enough to follow your dream and take the road less traveled.

Unfortunately for many, their dreams have become nightmares. In an article published by Forbes.com, 20% of small businesses fail in their first year, 30% in their second year, and 50% don't survive to see their fifth year.[1] A staggering 70% of businesses never make it to their 10th birthday. That means that while 14% of the population start their own businesses, only 4.2% remain business owners. Lucky for you, you're reading this book.

It doesn't matter your age, nationality, sex, financial status, location, or your product or service—if you're the owner of a business, I know you. I specialize in helping people like you establish systems, processes, and ever-changing marketing techniques. I teach the art of delegation and how to invest time wisely so that businesses can grow. As a former educator, I have a passion to teach and instruct.

Every business starts somewhat like a person—an infant, if you will. You might start with one or two clients or with a Facebook page, or by selling products online or from your garage. Either way, you started off small with a dream and the talent necessary to deliver your offerings. The more people know, like, and trust you, the more you sell. If you're in the fortunate group of 80% of business owners who succeed in your first year, you move to the second.

---

[1] Article: https://www.forbes.com/sites/ellevate/2019/10/24/eight-common-reasons-small-businesses-fail/#534f2d14fbb5

However, fewer entrepreneurs make it through their second year. Based on percentages, fewer and fewer make it through the third year, the fourth, then the fifth. And, as previously stated, only 30% make it to the 10th year. Between year one and year ten, there's what I call the teenage stage. Your enterprise is no longer an infant. You've overcome some hurdles and you're still standing. Yet, like a teenager, you think you know more than you do. Or more accurately, you think you know all there is to know about running your business. That's the single biggest reason why businesses start to fail.

These businesses never mature to live up to the lofty, wildly profitable dreams their owners once had. The entrepreneurs in the 30% group who make it beyond that 10th year are those who know how to leverage what they don't know.

I live somewhere in between there. I help "teenage" businesses grow up in sales, systems, processes, awareness, and profitability. The "*Now what?*" Stage is where I thrive—the level where most entrepreneurs find themselves when they realize that they don't know what they don't know, and as a result, they're stuck. They did all they knew to do, but now their businesses have plateaued—or worse, started to decline.

Incredibly talented and passionate people—people much like yourself, most likely—who start a business realize that while they may be excellent at creating the product, selling the service, or delivering on the service, they weren't ready to start a business. They find that they don't know the first thing about how to pay their taxes properly, how best to handle a customer complaint, how to make a collection call to someone who owes money, what to look for in vendors or strategic partners, insurance, marketing, how to network effectively, and many other things a business needs to grow.

After all, you've gone from being an employee who did a specific job to having to do every job for a company. Not many people can make the necessary adjustments, which is why so many companies fail regardless of how well the owner knew how to deliver.

Like Socks on a Rooster

If you've started a business, odds are that you found a mentor who helped you through the highs and lows of your entrepreneurial journey. My dad—my #1 mentor and hero—had a saying whenever we accomplished something difficult. For example, when I was growing up, we rarely bought furniture. Whenever the house got *stale* and needed a shakeup, we would move the furniture to different areas. Usually, my father would have a tape measure and we would spend much time and effort moving every piece of furniture all over the living room until we finally got it to where everyone agreed that the arrangement made the room look better. Hands on hips while admiring his work, my father would say, "Like socks on a rooster." Meaning, it was difficult, but we got it done.

He said it so often that I thought it was a common saying. When I would say it to friends or while at college, people would look at me as if I had two heads.

I'd say, "You know... like socks on a rooster?"

Blank stares. I was dumbfounded.

"What? You don't say that where you're from?"

Apparently, my father invented the saying, or up until know I've never met anyone else who knew of it. But running a successful business isn't easy—it's like putting socks on a rooster (Feel free to pass that on.) As we move through this journey, that saying, along with many others from my father and other mentors, will help unravel the mysteries of entrepreneurship that we all face.

Because running a business isn't easy, one important thing to do is celebrate small victories. Good sports coaches allow their teams to celebrate wins. But as soon as they leave to another stadium, they focus on the next task. In the business world, burnout is a real thing. Don't be the type of coach who withholds celebrating until you win a championship. Reward yourself with small victories. It will keep your motivation fed and wanting more.

Speaking of motivation, it's a tricky thing. As with just about everything else, it has its pros and cons. One of the cons is that it can be a false positive—meaning that you might feel you're at the tipping point of great things happening but that tipping over moment never comes. Just so you know, I'm a big fan of the self-help/motivational movement. I've gone to conferences, workshops, taken online courses, read books on it; I've been there, got the t-shirt. But it's important to understand this truth: motivation by itself is a deadly disease.

Without proper systems in place, motivation can keep someone holding onto their dream long enough to ruin their marriage, their family, their credit, mortgages, health, and their most important relationships. Motivation isn't tangible. It's a feeling that only you will feel. You might wake up optimistic every morning to get to work, and it's wonderful to feel that way, but if your sales never reflect your optimism, then delusion has probably set in.

Entrepreneurship is a lonely venture. When you were at your previous jobs, you were involved in a specific society or social structure. You had colleagues; people you went to lunch with, talked sports with, debated politics with, or maybe even fell in love with or hated. Then you start your business, working from a home office, a coffee shop, or renting an office in a shared business complex and you find yourself alone. Not necessarily lonely but alone in making decisions on what to spend time on, what task to do next, what to spend money on, and whether you should quit now and get a real job again. I'm here to tell you, the road of entrepreneurship doesn't have to be walked by yourself. As a business owner, you are a part of a vast, intelligent, motivated, and talented network. You just have to know how to tap into it.

In this book, you'll find answers you've been searching for as well as answers to questions you didn't even know to ask. At the end of the day, it's up to you to manifest what you learn here into action. Knowledge by itself, like motivation by itself, can hurt more than help. However, if you apply what I teach here, the same systems, processes, teachings, and truths I've used to take six-figure companies into million-dollar companies, you'll be able to help many more people, which will change the trajectory of your life.

Achieving entrepreneurial success isn't easy, but once you do, it sure is rewarding. When everything is in place and you see your business grow up, you will definitely say, "Like socks on a rooster!"

CHAPTER 2

MY STORY

Everyone has a story about how they began their entrepreneurial journey. Here's mine:

My wife had just had our first child, Michael Jr. It was the start of an amazing journey for my wife and me. In less than a year, I had gone from living on my own to living with a wife and a child. I'd never been a great student, but ironically, I was great at teaching.

How I came to be a teacher is something we'll get into later, but at the time my first son was born I was teaching ninth and tenth grade. It was the mid-2000s and I knew that using technology would be the best way to impact my students: I had a podcast, I was writing a blog, and I had a YouTube channel.

This creativity wasn't just creating a buzz in my classroom, but it also caught the eye of my principal, Ana Garcia. She told me that I was going to do great things in education! As I spoke to my fellow educators to figure out how to keep growing in my career, the answer I kept getting was pretty much the same: go back to school.

I loved teaching, but at that time, I hated school. Even so, I decided to get my master's in educational technology. I wanted to be able to tell my grandkids that I had been a part of the technological revolution in education.

My career plan was to work my way up to become an assistant principal, then a principal, and then maybe a superintendent. This was particularly crazy because I was a lousy student—at one point, getting out of school was all I cared about—and now I wanted to stay in for life.

Crazy worked, though, because I earned my master's at the same time my wife was pregnant. At about nine months pregnant with our second son, Anthony, I saw a job opening for an assistant principal for an online Catholic school where my primary responsibility would be to oversee their curriculum. The ad stated that everything had already been prepared—the content and the platform—the only thing the successful candidate would have to do was manage it.

While I was driving to the interview, my wife called.

"I think I'm having the baby!"

"Oh wow! Um, do you think I should cancel?"

"No, go ahead. I'm going to make some food for when you get back so we can go together."

Surprisingly, my interview went well, considering the distracting circumstances. Then the interviewer asked me, "How serious are you about this job?"

I answered. "Well, on my way here, my wife called to tell me that we're about to have our baby, and here I am."

Her mouth almost hit the floor. She said, "I appreciate your seriousness, but go home and take care of that!"

My family had now grown from a family of three to a family of four, and the principal called to inform me that I'd gotten the job.

So, there I was—I had a newborn at home and a stable job where everyone loved me—and I quit that job to go to another school so I could do a job I'd never done before. It seemed like a good idea, right? On paper, it was. Except once I started the job, it turned out that it wasn't the dream job they'd promised me. The curriculum was *not* all written, their LMS platform was unproven technology, and the principal fired the more experienced assistant principal who was supposed to mentor me during my first month on the job. I hadn't signed up for that. I panicked and probably experienced my first, and only, panic attack.

I called my former principal, Ana, to see if I could get my job back but to no avail. As I was focusing on managing the curriculum that didn't truly exist, the principal fired the person hired to do the sales and then explained to me that she didn't have the time to hire another and that I would have to go with her to Arizona for a big sales pitch where I would deliver the presentation.

I had previous sales experience at Circuit City, but I'd never done anything remotely close to giving a major boardroom presentation. But there I was speaking to a room full of principals. The presentation went so well that, in good old Catholic education style, she gave me two jobs: online curriculum and sales. Not backing down from the challenge, together we grew the product from coast to coast, signing up Catholic schools to use our online school.

Remember that unproven technology I mentioned earlier? That came from the principal's brother's company. He loved what I did in the Catholic education sphere, so he wanted to see if I could help his sales teams get the LMS into more public schools. I started helping her brother's company by selling the software to schools, but his goal was to find an investor for the business. We grew that product, expanded into 34 states, and we finally caught the attention of an investor, local south Florida billionaire, Wayne Huizenga, who also owned Blockbuster and the Miami Dolphins. I don't know how much he invested, but everyone who started in the grassroots at the company got new cars and started flying in his private Boeing 747 that had a living room where we held meetings before presentations.

From there, I've been privileged to travel on private planes and sit at 20-foot-long conference tables with leather chairs with some of the most powerful men and women sitting in them in expensive suits. A year before, I had been teaching in a classroom, and in what seemed like a blur, I was conducting business deals with millionaires and billionaires.

One time I flew first-class with a team to Nicaragua. On the way there, a few of us were informed we were going to a VIP's house to deliver a presentation. Once we deplaned and cleared customs, we got pulled to a room about the size of a school cafeteria and were ordered to present our passports again. We were handed champagne and water while we waited. After getting our passports back, three black Suburbans rolled up to bring us to the meeting. I couldn't help but notice the glaring contrast between the one who owned the Suburbans and the widespread poverty. We got to the house, which was surrounded by brick walls with barbed wire on top, and were led inside, passing two men with machine guns strapped around their necks.

"Where the hell are we?" I asked aloud.

"Oh, we're in Arnoldo Aleman's house, the former President of Nicaragua," was the reply.

I didn't know much about him, but I found out after the trip that he had earned a pretty bad reputation. (Ultimately, he would be convicted of corruption and sentenced to a 20-year term. Transparency International named him the ninth-most corrupt leader in recent history).

We had arrived on a Wednesday, and the meeting went so well he asked us to go to his private beach house as a guest on Friday. We enjoyed a private chef cooking us a seven-course meal followed by cigars and the finest scotch while overlooking the Pacific Ocean.

While I had thought the Nicaragua trip would be the start of a high point in my career with the growing company I almost left, it marked the end of the journey. As the saying goes, money changes everything.

Sadly, the rise to the top often gets mired in petty jealousies and burgeoning egos and there was a lot of tension amongst the management, including with my mentor and boss. It all came to a tipping point on Monday, May 7th. We had developed a huge global sales pipeline that was closing deals left and right when suddenly I was fired along with my boss. My boss told me later that I was collateral damage from the internal battles between him and the other owners of the company. I'd just come home from doing deals with a former national president, and now I was unemployed.

At that point, I had two options. One was the easy route: As it was May and jobs would be opening up for the next school year, I could have gone back to teaching. I was good at it, and I could leverage my recent experiences to rise through the ranks to superintendent even quicker. The second was the road less traveled: I could use my newfound experiences to help business owners grow.

That experience of getting fired shifted something in me—I never want to have that feeling of being fired again. I decided not to take the safe route and started assisting different start-ups in their growth. I started with solo-preneurs, then small companies, and eventually built my way up to becoming a high-priced consultant for several large companies.

As a former educator, I found a niche in developing employee trainings for large companies. I caught the eye of a company that trained employees of oil and gas companies. They offered me a million dollars for one project. Less than three years after I was fired, I had created a consulting business that was not only helping small businesses and startups but was in the process of going international, as I took a consulting job in Israel with a Fortune 1000 company. I couldn't believe that I, a former teacher, was sitting in these boardrooms or cruising on the Mediterranean to an oil rig. For this Italian boy, life had become quite surreal.

I remember my first time taking a ship to an oil rig in the middle of the ocean. Once you arrive, you have to get in a basket where a crane takes you far above the water. I remember looking at a security guard who was a former Israeli Soldier and asking him, "What do you do if you're scared of heights?"

The man deadpanned, "You're screwed."

As excited as I was about the biggest deal of my career, I learned quickly how easily a million dollars could be spent. I hired many people to expand my team, implemented robust trainings, and had to deal with many more moving parts than I could have imagined. Making the sales became easy; the hard part was in the implementation. I had to deal with different languages, different ideologies, and many 'you'd-better-put-the-fire-out-*now*' emergencies. One time I had to suddenly jump on a plane to Israel on Halloween to ensure the success of the project.

Mastering the implementation process became my passion. Being able to see things before they happen, maximizing people's talents, and logically planning out each progressive step became addicting to me. I've been helping business owners grow their businesses ever since by mastering the three areas that are key to growth and success: marketing, sales, and implementation. I hope to teach you more about how these areas impact your business, no matter the size or which stage of growth you're in.

CHAPTER 3

THINK DIFFERENT, BUT BE STRATEGIC

Ideas Are Easy

Growing up Catholic, I was told clear your mind and pray; God will talk to you. I have many friends who have said meditation is a great way to improve focus. For me, it's always been hard to clear my mind of everything because, even as a kid, I felt there was so much going on, and all these ideas would flood in! Human beings are thoughtful by nature. We couldn't *not* think if we tried. If you tried to clear your mind right now, you'd think on how you wouldn't be able to do it because you're thinking about clearing it rather than thinking about nothing.

When I was younger, I played t-ball, and I remember the coach and my dad yelling at me to stop daydreaming. Even today, I find my mind wandering with all the possibilities of how I can help make a client great, or a date night I want to go on with my wife, or the fun things I can do with my kids. Letting your mind wander is easy, it's taking your dreams and making them real that takes work. For me, I always thought this was a weakness until I started my journey as a business owner.

Entrepreneurs think differently. We think *big*! We focus on making the world better, whether one person at a time or in bunches. We spend a lot of time thinking about how we can provide a product or service to the masses. Getting the idea is easy. I've probably thought of 30 different businesses I could start. Ideas aren't the problem. Ask anyone, "If you were to start a business, what would it be?" I think 90% would answer right away, and the other 10% would answer a few minutes later. So, even though you've come up with a billion-dollar idea, it doesn't matter. Ideas alone don't make money; the money only comes with the execution.

It's a shame for those people who really do have great ideas and never act on them.

In fact, it's been said that cemeteries are the richest places on earth because that's where people have buried their ideas, and some of them could have transformed the world. Starting your own business takes courage, and sadly, not many have enough of it. But for you, the one who has acted on your idea and created your business, you're now beset on all sides about which things to do next:

Should I do a SWOT analysis?

Should I hire someone?

Should I start a podcast?

Should I start a YouTube channel?

Should I write a book?

Should I do some Facebook Live events?

Should I do this...

Should I do that...

Your problem might not be so much in execution (in that you're spending as much time as you can on your business). Your problem might be what to execute. There are two ways you can go. You can diversify—branch out and try to add services or products in order to serve more people, or you can niche down and work on being an expert to a specific category of people.

Both ways work when done right. However, if I had to choose between the two, I'm a big believer, as the great Judge Graham says, "There are riches in niches." People tend to think that if they niche down they're going to miss out on too many people. Let me remind you of this though: we're living in a time where there are more human beings on the planet than ever before. You can niche down to a specific group and still be able to serve millions of people.

The single best thing about niching down is that it's easier to be viewed as an expert to a specific group as opposed to a large one. For example, if you're a business coach, you may not have the funds or the desire to compete with Tony Robbins on a national or international level. However, if you are Boston's Best Business Coach who deals exclusively with companies with more than a million dollars a year in revenue, you'll have a much better chance of landing that type of client because that's where your expertise lies.

The truth is if building a successful business was easy, Forbes wouldn't be sharing that 87% of businesses crash and burn in the first five years. As my dad says, "If it were easy, everyone would be doing it!" For me, the best and worst thing about entrepreneurship is that you have options. I've always admired MLMs and franchises because they have a clear blueprint for you to follow as an entrepreneur. If you're just starting out with your own business with no real blueprint, or you're looking to "disrupt" an industry, the options could seem endless and it's hard to pick just a niche. To quote my father again, he often told me, "Don't worry about making the right decision. Pick a direction and *make* it right."

It's easy to give out motivating advice about riding out storms and not giving up, but it's hard when you're in the storm. It's hard when you've missed some payments and now you aren't even sure if you can buy groceries. It gets harder when non-business owners are quick to advise you to "get a real job." Everyone has an opinion, so part of your success depends on who you decide to listen to. It gets just as challenging when you start having success and people start telling you that it's time to branch out here or there. If you're in that situation where you've had some success and you're not sure how to scale or where to go, hire a business coach and/or mentor who has taken companies from where you are to where you want to go.

Motivation

Do you know what happens when you motivate an idiot?

You get a motivated idiot.

I'm not calling anyone names. I'm stating a fact. If you're motivated to learn how to make great lasagna, but you don't go online for a great recipe or ask anyone who makes great lasagna for his or her advice, your motivation to make a great lasagna bears nothing on the lasagna. People get motivated to become successful business owners the same way. Many business owners have jumped into their businesses with two feet. They've gone all-in from Day One but fall into the trap of 'FIRE! Ready... Aim...

They've envisioned themselves making $200K a year in three years and a million in seven. However, at year five, when the company is making $120K, they lose motivation. The desire for money, freedom, a boat, to travel, or whatever it may be doesn't materialize just because you're motivated. In fact, motivation has very little to do with success. I know millionaires who aren't motivated; they just got lucky on a business or idea. I also know a guy who started his own landscaping business out of necessity who now brings in upwards of a quarter-million dollars a year.

Don't get me wrong, motivation is needed for sure. But sometimes motivation without planning or process can be a detriment. It can keep you holding on to an idea that simply hasn't panned out. Sometimes when you lose your motivation, it's a sign to pivot—or it's the final nail in the coffin. I've seen motivated people stick around too long, only to be ruined financially and/or emotionally. I respect people with no-quit attitudes, but sometimes quitting is the right move.

Entrepreneurs have taken over the word *grind* as if grinding is winning. If you're continually on your grind, you're not winning. If you're *grinding* in the wrong area, you're hurting yourself more than helping. You need to learn. Before you start grinding away, it's imperative to first create a process. If you make 1,500 calls and each call is different, you may be on your grind, but your grind isn't working. Pivot doesn't always mean change the direction of your business, sometimes it means change your approach.

Be willing to do what it takes to make the business successful. At times, that may not be the things you like to do. Do them anyway. Sometimes running a successful business sucks. You need to embrace the process. If you don't like the process and it sucks, then you have to embrace the suck—or outsource the suck.

It Takes More Than Work

The bar for entrance to entrepreneurship is incredibly low. It's literally just a couple hundred bucks to start a business. Anyone can get in. But getting in wasn't the goal for you, was it? If your goal as a quarterback is to win the Super Bowl, tossing a football around on Thanksgiving with your friends, even though it's the same exact motion, won't hit your goal. To play in the Super Bowl takes serious talent and a great work ethic, great coaching, following an optimized process, and a little bit of luck. In the same vein, to become successful in business takes passion, talent, work ethic, mentorship, and having a process—and a little bit of luck.

It's not true that all you have to do is work hard. In fact, I'd rather you not work at all for a week and develop the right plan/strategy/process. If you do that, you'll easily pass those who worked on their grind during the week that you worked on your process. We need to stop believing some of these motivational quotes as words to live by. Blindly working hard can kill your business.

At one time, Blockbuster was the dominant company in the home movie space. I remember as a kid going to Blockbuster and renting movies for family movie night. It was a great experience. Many people talk about how Blockbuster failed and how Netflix destroyed them. One of the first startups I worked with was invested in by Wayne Huizenga, the founder of Blockbuster Video. He sold Blockbuster long before society outgrew them. The lesson I learned from Wayne and his team is this: you have to know when the time has come to let go. They were actually going to buy Viacom and could have *become* Netflix, but they knew that this wasn't at the core of their business, so they flipped the script and sold Blockbuster to Viacom for $8.4 billion and moved on to the next successful venture. The lesson here is that you have to know when to let go and move on.

Sears was also king of the castle at one time. The Sears catalog was a must-have for millions of people. As a business, if your brand made it to the Sears catalog, you were set! Amazon thought people could just buy things from home. It would eliminate many overhead expenses so people could get the products they like cheaper. Well, Sears is no longer is no longer king, and Amazon is one of the largest businesses in the world. Did Sears fail and Amazon succeed, or did the world just change?

Motivation is not a bad thing; it's sorely needed. But I'm busting the stereotype that working hard is what will make you successful. Blockbuster and Sears didn't fail due to lack of hard work; it was the environment around them that changed. To be a successful business owner, motivation is a very small piece of the pie. Give me a good process and solid consistency, and I'll outsell a motivated, hard worker every time.

Talent, salesmanship, feedback, process, and a little bit of luck are the keys to success in entrepreneurship. Now, let's turn those keys and drive.

CHAPTER 4

YOUR STORY

One of the major problems entrepreneurs face (owners of smaller business who either work by themselves, for themselves, or those who employ less than 50 people) is not getting enough of the right attention.

First, let's talk Business 101: Your business needs attention. People need to know that you're in business in order for them to potentially buy from you. So, we market ourselves to the degree to which we're able. We have our websites, our business cards, and we post on social media. That's what most entrepreneurs do. When we go out and we're asked, "What do you do?" we tell them about the business we run. We rarely tell them how it helps others, but that's very important. But what's even worse is that we don't tell them *why* we do what we do.

The Importance of Your Story

For years, I've spoken to, interviewed, worked with, and collaborated with business owners. I've met tons of them. I've noticed that when people start to talk about what they do, they'll talk about the fact that they don't work for anyone else and they own their own business. They say it with a sense of pride, and they may not even realize it, but they stand up a little taller.

That is, until I ask my next question.

"Why?"

It always seems as if the question throws them off guard, as if they weren't prepared to answer it. Maybe they were just hoping that I'd nod and ask them about their product, service, or price. I don't because most of the time I have a good idea about those answers since I know similar companies. What confuses me is that it confuses them. After all, they're the only ones who can answer that question!

We buy from people we feel we know, like, and can trust (you will see this phrase repeated because I want it to sink in). Chances are, you aren't the only one who does what you do: you're not the only landscaping company, you're not the only restaurant that specializes in breakfast, you're not the only lawyer, the only realtor, the only business coach, life coach or health coach, the only banker, barber, hairstylist, or dentist. So, why not take advantage of meeting me and let me know *why* you do what you do so that I can feel as if I know you a little more, start to like you more than as a person I just met, and begin to feel like I can trust you a little more with my hard-earned money or the people I can refer to you.

Why did you start your business? What's *your* story?

Did you get fired after putting a ton of work into someone else's business? Did you have a bad experience and quit a job you once thought you'd work at for many years? Did you always dream of providing the type of service you're providing ever since you were a kid, or during high school, during the military, or during college? Did you have a chance meeting with someone who inspired you? Did you run out of money and think of a way to make more? Did you see a need and figure out a way to fill it? Did someone close to you suffer from something and you vowed to help others to never be in that position again? What was it? What's your why? What's your story?

Depending on what you sell and who you're interacting with, there are times when it's hard to sell people. They may not always be in the market for your product or service. But that doesn't mean you can't lay the groundwork for them to remember you when they do need what you do. If you can't sell people, stay in front of them and tell them your story.

I know people whose businesses have failed, people who've been in business for 5, 7, or 12 years—and when their businesses failed, no one cared. That wasn't the market's fault; it was the owners' fault.

Many business owners don't talk much about the *why* because they're worrying or concentrating on the *where*. In other words, they forget why they started the business and focus on where the business is going. I understand that rationale. But I have to tell you, it's flawed. In order to get to where you want to go, there's going to be bumps along the road, maybe even stop signs or detours, which means it may take a while to get to where you want to go. The *why* needs to be your fuel!

If you started a business because you loved doing something and after several years, the work is hard and you're not being appreciated or paid well, your love for the task that your business is set up for starts to wane. Without the *why,* you run out of passion, and passionless business owners wind up being someone's employee because more often than not, their business fails.

So, share your story. Put it on your website. Create a video and post it on Facebook. Create a blog post about it put it on LinkedIn. Tweet about it. Do an image montage and put it on Instagram. Talk about it at your next networking event. Stop promoting your business and start promoting the passion behind it.

When You Don't Share Your Story

One of the stereotypes this book destroys is this one: "My haters are going to fuel me!" As if it were that easy. Sorry to bust your bubble, but your haters aren't even talking to you, they're talking to your prospects and potential customers. They're helping people form their opinions about you, and if these people don't know your story, they're going to believe what your haters tell them.

"He opened up a restaurant with no restaurant experience!" (Not knowing that your parents had a restaurant that you worked at for 12 years before going away to college).

"She just got her license and opened a brokerage without knowing what it's like to be an agent." (Not knowing that your mother was a top-producing agent for 20 years and is working with you.)

They aren't your haters, they're your narrators. You've granted them the ability to speak for you through your silence.

When you don't share your story, your competition will tell it for you. And naturally, they're going to tell their version of your story. It may not even be their intention to lie about you, but they'll take what little truth they know, build their own story around it, and pass it off as your story so that they can get more business.

People telling your story for you don't necessarily have to be competitors. They could be people in your own family or inner circle—people who recommended against open your own business because they're afraid to take risks; now they're upset that you're moving on, so consciously or unconsciously, they're hoping you'll fail.

Start With Why—Keep it Going

In this era of film sagas (case-in-point: The Star Wars franchise with nine movies, some animated series, and another series, *The Mandalorian*, now showing on Disney+), it's not only important to tell your story but also to continue to share your story as it develops and be able to share it on multiple platforms. Netflix and all the major television networks also continue to create more content on shows that are successful. Not only should you share your why, but also share what's happening.

One of the ways to continue to share your story is to celebrate victories, even some that may seem small. Every time you bring in a staff member, even if it's for a few hours a week, share it. Every time you have a record-breaking month, you don't want to disclose your earnings, but share the milestone. Every time your company is selected to participate in something or you decide to become a sponsor for something you're passionate about, share it. Celebrate your victories and allow others to celebrate them with you. What I'm saying is this: it's much easier to stay in business with people who feel as if they know you, like you, and can trust you when you've leveraged these natural stories to the point that they're rooting for you.

In being authentic with your story, there may be times when things get tough, or you may need to refer back to a time when they were tough. I understand that one of the key selling points on how to sell is to come from a position of authority, from a position of strength. For this reason, many people don't like to or want to share times that weren't great. But showing vulnerability is a strength that few possess. Let's face it, if two people or teams that we are not emotionally attached to compete, we all like to cheer for the underdog.

Instead, people would rather not share their stories of vulnerability. "I'll fake it 'til I make it," they say. That's another stereotype I want to dismantle because it's dangerous to believe in that saying 100 percent. I get the saying; I just don't want you relying on it. That saying implies that you'll keep doing what it is you're doing until you make it. That may not be a good thing. Conveying understanding about your vulnerability (your weaknesses, if you will), allows you a golden opportunity to pivot some of your attention or resources into strengthening that weakness.

If you want others to think you're bigger than you are, I get it. But if your idea of faking it in any way entails not being able to deliver what you're saying you can, you're not going to make it.

Take, for example, someone who starts a digital marketing agency and says they're going to fake it 'til they make it...

In-house, they are strong at creating strategy, images, video, and web design. What they're not good at is content creation. But they've decided to fake it 'til they make it. Inevitably, clients that need strong content are not going to have a good experience with them. That's not merely going to result in not getting repeat business but also in having that client potentially telling others not to use that marketing agency at all. Now, if the digital marketing agency founder didn't believe in the fake it 'til they make it philosophy and instead partnered with an outside source who could deliver strong written content, there's nothing to fake, and they can just make it!

When you're true with your story—its origin, its successes, its vulnerabilities, and more successes, more people will develop an association with your brand. If you have two coffee shops across the street from each other with equally good coffee but you know that the person who owns one of the shops is former military and hired former military personnel who'd become homeless, which coffee would you buy more? The one whose story you know!

Stories, like songs, are easy to remember and share. People will forget the taste of a pastry, the flavor of a drink, the punctuality of a plumber, or the fact that their realtor took them to 20 different houses... but they won't forget *who they are* if they are told their stories.

Your Story Doesn't Have to Stay About You

One of the essential ways of growing a business is by duplicating oneself. When you get to a point where you're hiring, don't simply talk about the requirements for the job and the tasks that need to be performed. Tell the applicants your story. Show them your passion for what you do. Tell them some success stories of how you've helped others. Make your story their battle cry.

"So, you're looking for a secretary?"

"Yes and no. The person we hire will do a lot of tasks associated with a secretary, but we're looking for someone who has a heart for ____________. Let me share with you *why* I started my company"

Every business owner wants to build a winning culture. Let's look at Major League Baseball, where there are many great teams. They all play the same game with the same rules with the same equipment and for the same number of innings. Yet, the New York Yankees, love them or hate them, have a different culture. They have a rich legacy of bigger-than-life stars and more championships than any other team. Great players would accept less money to be a part of that franchise, to be a part of that lore, that legacy, that story.

When you share your story with your employees, whether they are subcontracted or not and whether they work with you in your office or from across the country, they get to add onto it. Now, they get out there and tell your story, but in their own way. They tell people how your passion ignited them to take the job, how your vision is going to help so many people, and how your expertise is going to set them up for life.

By now, you should be thinking of your story and probably even deciding on how best to tell it. Again, I want to focus on the why. This time, from the benefit of someone other than you or your business. You may not even know it, but people are looking at you. You may be the only entrepreneur in your family, and your kids, your siblings, parents, nieces and nephews are looking at you. There may be people who grew up with you who see you go out to make your dream come true. You might even inspire someone you'll never meet to go after his or her own dreams.

Where?

Don't just tell your story in one manner. There are many ways for business owners to communicate, and I want you to take advantage of all of them, or at least the Four Pillars of Storytelling:

1. Book
2. Podcast
3. Social Media
4. Online Course

People learn differently and associate in different settings, so cover all your bases. I'm excited to be sharing these four pillars with you as you get deeper into the book. But for right now, focus on your story—*why* you started your business—and plan on sharing it.

CHAPTER 5

I FAILED FIRST GRADE

Up to this point, we've been talking a lot about entrepreneurship and my 30,000-foot view of it, but I think it's important for you to understand my journey into entrepreneurship, and my *why*. It all started, as many great things did, in the 1980s!

Some say that being born in 1980 makes me a part of the last great generation. We were the last group to play outside from sunrise to sunset and the first to get bit by the digital bug. That being said, during my younger years, "hustle" was a word rarely heard outside of PE class, and success was something only people with good grades achieved. Growing up, I was neither an athlete nor a good student, but these words would come to define me. They led me on a journey that had me flying on private planes, working side-by-side with millionaires and billionaires, and taught me the life lesson of how fleeting success and failure can be.

I Failed First Grade

It was the summer of 1986, and it was one of the best summers ever because I'd received a Nintendo for my birthday in May. As summer came to a close, I got in as much kickball as I could with my friends during the day, while Mario and I tried to rescue the princess at night!

Each night before bed, my dad would come in and we would talk and say prayers. This warm August night was different, as even at six years old, I saw a different look in my dad's eyes.

He asked me, "Mike are you excited to go back to school next week?"

With the youthful optimism only a kid can have, I said, "Of course!"

I couldn't wait to tell everyone about all the video games I played. As I held Tafoo, my stuffed bear, Dad asked me, "What do you think about not going to second grade and doing first grade again?"

I said, "That sounds great. We played with Legos a lot, and that sounds like fun!"

To this day, I tell people I got my master's degree in Legos!

As a parent today, I can imagine that was a difficult conversation for my dad to have with me, but he always made me feel supported. My mom explained that it was a growing year, but being 5'5" today, I guess it didn't work! That being said, they couldn't have been more supportive of me, but this is when I first realized that I wasn't good at school. I will say that my mom and dad always tried to do what was best for me and pushed me. My mom even got a job at the school in the office, which was really cool when I needed lunch money, but not so cool when I got in trouble!

This Year Is Going to Be Different!

I was super excited for the decade to change to 1990 for two main reasons: first, I was going to turn double digits, and second, *Super Mario Brothers 3* was coming out that year! My parents were going to a party at a friend's house to ring in the new year, and we were allowed to go and stay up till midnight! This was the first time I remember doing this, as we'd usually stayed at my grandparents' house, or my parents made my sister and me go to sleep wherever the party was.

As I drank RC Cola and ate Publix cookies to stay awake, the clock struck midnight and everyone cheered, hugged, and sang. My sister had fallen asleep in the other room, but I was going strong like a real double-digit kid! As the excitement moved on, my dad sat me down and asked if I was excited. I was like, "I can't believe it's 1990; that is so cool!" He told me that this was going to be a great year, and he was going to do something different that would hopefully benefit our family greatly.

Little did I know that this would be my first experience with entrepreneurship. My dad joined Amway, a network marketing business. Now, I couldn't tell you what my dad did for a living by day when I was a kid. If people asked about my dad, I would tell them that he's Italian, wears a suit to work, and flies to New York once a month for business. Needless to say, no one ever tried to steal my lunch money! Later in life, I learned that he developed property management software.

I always knew my dad worked hard, but when he joined Amway, I learned things like "Fired-Up," "If time and money were no object, what would you do?" and "Get out and show the plan!" The concepts of goal setting and chasing a dream were really neat for me to see first-hand as a 10-year-old. I remember my parents having meetings at our house with people from everywhere, and I would watch my dad show the plan. I could finally tell people what my dad did for a living. He showed the plan, did business with our friends and family, and flew to New York once a month!

That summer, my Uncle John and Aunt Janet came down from New Jersey to visit. My parents had to attend a function for Amway out of town, so I stayed at my grandparents' house along with my uncle and aunt.

One morning at breakfast, Aunt Janet asked me, "What is this Amway thing your parents are in?"

I replied, "Well, Aunt Janet, let me ask you a question. If time and money were no object, what would you do?"

After a good amount of laughter from everyone at the breakfast table, she said "What do you mean?"

I told her she should let me show her. I grabbed a legal pad and began to show her the plan just as I'd seen my dad do so many times.

Needless to say, when my parents returned, my uncle and aunt asked them how they could sign up. Not only did my dad and his brother get to work together on the business thanks to me, but it was also one of the most successful legs in their organization. That simple breakfast became a key story in my family's life. It was the first time I felt the rush of the hustle and the joy of success.

Miami Dolphins, #1

The Christmas of 1991 brought a really cool gift from Santa, the Super Nintendo! I was excited, and really enjoyed playing it over the winter break. Once again, we rang in the new year, and my dad and I were due for another heart-to-heart talk about what 1992 would bring. Thanks to my hustle and prospecting skills, my parents' network marketing business was growing. They were being mentored by their up-line, Tim Foley, former Miami Dolphins player from the 1972 undefeated season. This was a really cool experience, as I got to see the dream and the goal become a reality. Tim was a big guy. He had a big house, a big car, a big boat, and a big heart. Growing up in an average middle-class neighborhood, this was really cool for me to see!

Fast forward a year and I had completed my Cub Scout career with Pack 675 and was moving on to Boy Scout Troop 118. This was really cool for two reasons: first, I got to be around older kids who could teach me cool stuff. Not having a brother, this was something I'd always wanted. The second thing was that I had another Miami Dolphin from the 1972 undefeated team as one of our scout masters, Manny Fernandez.

As a kid and a football fan, it was so cool to be so close to both Tim and Manny, and their message was always the same—work hard in school, listen to your parents, and do your best. The last two were no problem, but the first one was still so hard for me to achieve. Back then, I couldn't progress in school as I would've liked. Even moving into middle school, I still struggled and asked myself, "What will I be able to do as an adult? How will I be successful?"

The Phone Call That Changed Everything

The summer of 1994 was amazing. It was my last year in middle school, and I was getting ready to head to high school. At this point, video games were a thing of the past, and I had moved on to more interesting activities. Cars, girls, music, and having a good time were on my mind. As I quickly learned, everyone was hungry on the bus ride home, so I sold candy at school to make extra cash. I would take my new-found wealth and head straight to Publix to get more candy for the next day, and Al's Baseball Cards to get a deck of cards with my profit.

My parents were still killing it in the network marketing business. My dad finally achieved the pinnacle of success all Italians strive for: he bought a Cadillac! This was so cool, and I thought, *Wow, this is going to be my first car!* It wasn't, but we will get to that. My dad and mom were asked to speak about their network marketing success all over the U.S. and the Caribbean. This was very impressive to me, and I really enjoyed watching videos of them speaking. When they spoke locally, I would try to go watch and soak it all in. I said, "I want to do that someday."

Then, one Friday night in September, the phone rang right before my bedtime. My mom answered and yelled to my father that the phone was for him. She had a concerned look on her face. My dad grabbed the phone as my mom told my sister and me to head to bed. As I listened from my room, I could hear my dad saying the common phrases when you know something is wrong: "Oh my God, are you serious? Wow, what can we do?" He said them over and over.

The next morning, I had a Boy Scout event that my dad had to drive me to. My father looked as if he hadn't slept, and we both got into the Cadillac very quietly that morning. Much like he had four years earlier on New Year's Eve, he said the same words, but much differently.

"That phone call last night changed everything for our family," he said.

"Why is that?"

"My boss passed away, and there's no one left to run the company. This next year is going to be different."

My dad was now in a position where he had a choice. He could go full-time into network marketing, or he could take over the small four-man company that he worked for. After much deliberation, my dad decided to take over the small company he'd worked for. While I'd seen my parents work hard in network marketing, this would be my first glimpse of high-level success. My dad was going to be the boss! I could finally tell people what my dad did for a living! He was Italian, drove a Cadillac, and was the boss! Needless to say, I still didn't have a problem with people stealing my lunch money as my academic career advanced!

The Law of Multiplication

The summer of 1995 brought some unfortunate news as my grades weren't where they should be, and my social activity was increasing. My parents felt it was time for me to leave the public school system and head to private school. This was not something I was excited about, as I had friends I'd grown up with for many years moving on to the brand new public high school up the street from us. I also thought it would be way harder for me academically in private school.

So, with my beeper in my pocket and my too-cool-for-school attitude, I headed up the walkway of Chaminade Madonna College Preparatory. Two things really surprised me on day one. First, was that we had the worst uniforms and second, not everyone was like me and had come from public school. Many of the kids had gone to private school together for their whole lives. As I walked into the cafeteria for freshman orientation, I spotted a group of kids I knew from our public school. There were about 10 of us at that table. By the end of the first month, only five of us were left.

My mom, while not letting me go to the public high school, did get a job there. She came home one day after the first week of school and said, "Hey, a new burger place just opened across the street called Char-Hut and they want to hire some high school kids. I told the owner you'd be perfect."

I did kind of want to be a chef, so I was like, "Okay, I'll take a walk over there."

It was right next to Al's Baseball Cards anyway, and private school kids also liked buying candy after school.

I went into the newly built restaurant and told them I was there to apply for a job. I met Jeff, the manager. He was a tall, skinny guy with a hamburger ring and a southern accent. He gave me an application to fill out. In my best doctor handwriting I filled out as much as I could, but when it asked about prior work experience, I had to leave it blank.

"You never worked anywhere?" Jeff asked.

"I sold candy on the bus to kids." I answered, and Jeff laughed.

"Oh, you're a Boy Scout?" he said.

"Yes, sir." I replied.

"Okay," he said. "You start on the fryer tomorrow night. Here's your uniform."

The first night I worked was like nothing I'd ever seen before. Jeff had his Hamburger Ring all shined up and was ready to go. When I walked in, he gave me my timecard and walked me to the fryer. He asked if I was ready for my training and I told him I was.

He said, "When we yell, 'Three-piece,' you put three chicken fingers in the fryer. Make sure we've got fresh french fries all night, and don't burn yourself. Got it?"

I told him I did, with what I presume was fear in my eyes. As the night went on, everything just started happening faster and faster, and I got more and more confused. About halfway through, I got into a rhythm, and out of nowhere Jeff, holding a spatula in one hand and a grill fork in the other, let out a loud whoop and told me I'd got it. Man, that feeling of success at picking something up on my own was contagious.

At the end of the shift, Jeff called me into the office and asked how the first night went.

I said, "You tell me."

He laughed and told me I'd done well and that I would be paid $3.75 an hour for the first month, then $4.15 an hour after that. Then he asked if I had a girlfriend and I told him that I didn't.

He said "Son, let me tell you, something. When you get one, your movie tickets are going to be twice as expensive. Then if you marry one of them girls and have a kid, your movie tickets will be three times as expensive. You seem like a hard worker, but I am going to tell you this: work hard in school, listen to your parents, and do your best."

You WILL Do Something Different

I spent most of my high school career working at Char-Hut. It provided me a good stream of money, and I worked my way up to cashier. I liked that because I went home smelling less like a french fry. I was able to save up enough to get my first car in 1997. It was a 1985 powder blue Mercury Marquise—*not* the Cadillac. Her name was Blue Thunder. I put blue Christmas lights under the dash and two 15-inch subwoofers in the trunk.

With the exception of getting my new car at the beginning of my junior year, each year of high school was about the same. Halfway through the quarter, I would have Ds and Fs, the school would let my parents know, and I would hustle my way to Cs and Ds. After two-and-a-half years of this, my parents had had enough. They went to talk to both the president and the principal of the school.

The principal, Bob Minnaugh, was also my Geometry teacher. The first day of class, he walked in and exclaimed, "If you want to make it in life, you have to sell yourself!"

I laughed at this at first, but to this day, that saying is still with me. You could say Mr. Minnaugh was a visionary, as social media teaches us today that personal branding, telling your story, and selling yourself can help you 10x your business.

The day after my parents met with them, the president of the school, Brother John Campbell, called me to his office. Keep in mind that in three years of being in the school I hadn't been involved much and I'd really never spoken to him. I expected a "do your best speech," but he said something completely different.

He asked me, "Mike, what do you want to be when you grow up?"

I told him, "Maybe a chef, but I honestly don't know."

Brother Campbell told me that whatever I did for a living wouldn't be based on what I learned in the classroom or on my grades, but it *would* be based on my personality and hard work. He went on to describe school as a process you have to go through to become well-rounded, but said that my path would be different, and that that was okay.

He asked me if I wanted to make my parents proud. "Of course," I replied. Then he asked who my favorite teacher was. I told him that I thought my history teacher, Mr. Eimmerman, was pretty cool; it was his first year teaching. Brother Campbell told me to see Mr. Eimmerman after school—he would be my mentor.

This was the first time I'd heard the word mentor, and it would change my life. Jim Eimmerman ended up being a lifelong friend and mentor who eventually guided me to my first job in education. After that meeting, I really fell in love with the high school that earlier I couldn't wait to get kicked out of. I went on to graduate with a solid C average and even became prom king!

Congratulations! You Have Been Accepted to Broward Community College!

All of us have said to ourselves, *"If I could do it over again, I would do things differently."* As my senior year of high school came around, many of my friends started to apply to colleges throughout the state of Florida. As I spoke with my counselor, she kindly told me that it might be best for me not to apply and just do two years of community college. This was really tough for me to hear as I saw many of my friends going away. I went on a trip with some of them to visit the University of Central Florida (UCF) in Orlando Florida, and I fell in love with the place. I went home and filled out an application. Before the stamp was practically even stuck to the envelope, I got a rejection letter. Apparently, prom king didn't pull a lot of weight with the admissions office.

So, that summer I partied with all my friends and watched them leave, one-by-one. Outgrowing the Char-Hut job and no longer wanting to be a chef, I started looking for another job. I applied at Circuit City and was hired in the cell phone department. This was 1999 and you could get a phone for $0.01 with a one-year contract, but the warranty was where the real money was made. My first night working I sold more phones than I could remember. I figured that this was it. I'd found my place.

The next morning, I walked into the break room and my manager, Billy Hughes, was writing on a giant white board. He said, "Hey, Mr. Mike, great first day. You had the highest sales last night, way to sell that cheese!" Cheese is what they called the warranty, and coming from Char-Hut, I knew that was extra!

While I loved working in retail, I took off one weekend a month to visit my friends up at UCF. I couldn't wait to get up there and go to school. My time at Broward Community College (BCC), much like high school, wasn't my best: solid Cs and Ds in most classes was still the norm. I was making a lot of money selling the cheese, but I had that goal of getting into UCF. I also changed my major about 10 times, everything from psychology to accounting to marketing. It was a moving target, but I did it, and finished in two years. As I graduated from community college with my AA, my sister who was much smarter than me was graduating from high school with a full scholarship to UCF. I, on the other hand, had just gotten in, but I was excited!

Failure Is Part of Success

As we drove up to UCF, I felt like a kid in a candy store. My parents moved my sister into the dorms, and I got an apartment with some friends I'd met at BCC. That night, as my parents were getting ready to make the four-hour drive back home to South Florida, my dad had that same look he'd had back in 1986 when we talked about doing first grade again. I asked him if he was okay, and he said, "I just hope you do your best and are able to take advantage of this opportunity." We hugged with tears in our eyes, and I watched them drive off thinking I would be fine.

My first semester was great. I had a job, an apartment, and I'd finally made it to the University of Central Florida campus. The problem was that I didn't make it to class. For a multitude of reasons, I had mostly Ds and Fs during my first semester, and as I came home for Christmas break, I was put on academic probation. When my grades became available online on New Year's Eve, my dad and I sat down and had another one of our talks at midnight, and he said he thought I should pack it up and come home. I told him that I could do it, and he told me I would have to do it on my own and pay my own way.

"Fair enough," I said, and headed back up to UCF. By the end of my second semester, my grades hadn't improved, and I was asked to leave the University of Central Florida. I moved back home.

Not knowing what I wanted to do, I decided to take a year off and work. I was waiting tables, and who walked in but Mr. Eimmerman! Jim and I exchanged numbers and agreed to get together for lunch. Not more than a few days later, he called me and said he was teaching Theology at the new Catholic high school, and they needed a substitute teacher. I thought it sounded like fun. I'd enjoyed high school.

After a few weeks substituting and being the cool young teacher, the librarian who was pregnant was put on bed rest. The principal called me in, told me that she would be out for the rest of the year, and asked me if I wanted to fill in for her. So, by default, I was the hottest 22-year-old librarian in the United States! I didn't want to be a librarian, but I fell in love with working in education. I went back to school to finish my degree in psychology and began teaching at the high school. Jim played a key role in mentoring me on how to be a great teacher. In addition, due to my fancy new teacher salary, I was able to reach that pinnacle all Italians strive for: I bought a used Cadillac!

Turns Out I Was Your Stereotypical Entrepreneur All Along

I remember always feeling like a loser due to having bad grades in school. I never felt like the hustle I had outside the classroom selling candy, working, or even getting my Eagle Scout badge mattered. Fast forward to the present, everyone from Gary Vaynerchuck, Grant Cardone, Tony Robbins, to the latest start-up, is led by a guy who hadn't gotten good grades while attending school. Where was this entrepreneur group when I was in school?

After getting my master's degree in Educational Technology (yes, the D student got a master's degree), I worked with EdTech startups across the country. I've had the privilege of working alongside A students, fellow D students, billionaires, millionaires, and even a few who went into debt in those directions as well. As an entrepreneur, I've also been involved in starting several businesses outside the EdTech space based on my success there. Working in fields such as telecommunication, oil and gas, manufacturing, incident investigation, and real estate has taught me that no matter the industry, if you study, work hard, and do your best, you will be able to find the path to success.

Over the years, I've seen great success and failure, but one thing that never changes is that I never stop learning. All my hard work even let me purchase my dream home for my family. I bought my dream Italian car, a Cadillac Escalade, and I have a beautiful wife and four children. Today, my kids can't really tell their friends what I do for a living, but they do tell them that their dad hustles, he's the boss, and he drives a Cadillac! Needless to say, they don't have the problem of people stealing their lunch money.

My wife always says to me, "No matter what you do, you're always hustling."

When I was teaching, I would stay up late planning my lessons for the next day to make sure they were new and exciting. When I worked for my first start-up, I traveled the country to help secure an investment that would allow us to take the company to the next level. When my wife and I started our family, I made sure that I did everything I could to ensure my kids would not experience some of the same struggles I did in school. My best advice? Marry a smart woman!

All that being said, I have learned that my journey couldn't have been a different one. If I'd been a great student, maybe I wouldn't have become such a hard worker. If my parents hadn't forced me into situations I was unhappy with, I wouldn't have ended up where I am today, helping businesses and entrepreneurs grow their organizations. If you look up the word *hustle* in the dictionary, it's described as both a noun and verb, but hustle is truly a *journey*. I hope my story has made you realize that you're never alone on that journey. Always remember these key concepts as you continue this book:

1. You *are not* defined by where and when you were born.
2. You *are not* defined by your failures.
3. You *are* who you surround yourself with.

CHAPTER 6

PARTNERSHIPS AND PROFITS

People usually become entrepreneurs one of two ways. Those who want to make something of themselves by owning their own company and those who start a business accidentally.

Most likely, those who intentionally started a business couldn't stop talking about opening their business one day. Then with professional license in hand or college degree under their belt—or after working for someone else long enough—they open their own business and achieve that goal of becoming an entrepreneur.

Those who accidentally started a business probably got there by selling something on the side (a side-hustle) that became so lucrative that it just made sense to put all their effort into it. These people started making money before having a website, a business account, business cards, or a Facebook page. This also includes those who were told they were good at a thing: arts & crafts, giving advice, baking cakes, etc., and opened a business at the behest of their peers.

Regardless of how you started, the odds are that you started your business by doing most, if not all, of the work yourself. However, now you have a burning desire to grow or scale your business. You've tasted success and you want more of it. You've helped some people, but you want to help more. You've been told that your business is awesome, you've been referred to others, you've steadily built your client list—and as a result, your business bank account—and now you want more people to know about it.

Now, you may think that you've already reached your goal: you own your own business and you're making enough money to be content—and maybe you have. However, if you're working from sunup to sundown and you're making money, in all reality, you're just paying yourself your own salary. Making enough money to live on does not, in my book, constitute having a successful business. It just means that you stopped working for someone else (a boss) to work for many bosses (your customers). That's not financial freedom. *Real* profits materialize when you're *not* trading time for money. This is where partnerships become so important.

The baby entrepreneurs will take the world on by themselves. They'll tell you, with pride, how they laugh at the work ethic of those who work 40 hours a week and how it can't compare to the 90 hours a week they work. They'll boast about how they're always grinding or how they have a no-quit mentality. They're always burning the midnight oil and working while others are sleeping. Five years later, they're still there, outworking everyone around them, but they're not growing. Don't get me wrong, every entrepreneur, particularly in the beginning, should invest a lot of time into their business. However, the idea is to *invest* those hours, not for that workload to become a new lifestyle.

At the end of the day, you want to get those hours back. You want to build a business that makes enough money so that you *don't* have to work yourself to the bone. You want to get those hours back to do the things you love, whether that's spending time with your family, going on vacations, or sitting down in front of your big screen television eating ice cream. When you're able to live a life that *you* design, you're not just making money, you're making profits. In order to get there, you're inevitably going to have to bring in other people.

Be Strong Where I'm Weak

As you go through ups and downs, a few defeats and some victories, you come to realize what you're good at, what you're not so good at, and what you're absolutely terrible at. For example, if you run a marketing agency, maybe you've realized that you're amazing at creating the strategy and you're great at sales, but you're not a great (or even a decent) designer. To your surprise, you may have found that you're much better at writing copy than you gave yourself credit for but not so good at the accounting aspect of your business. With self-realization comes clarity; the type of clarity that successful businesses are founded upon.

If you're going to bring others in, find people who are strong where you're weak. Bringing someone into your business is a big deal. The wrong person can ruin you, while the right person might seem out of your price range. It can even make you feel like you're financially going backwards. For example, if you're making $100K a year and the right accountant is going to cost your $40K a year, are you going forwards or backwards? Well, if it can help you make a million in three years, it's not so much going backwards as it is backing up to get some running room to jump farther. If you feel like life is great at the $100K your business makes and you're happy where you are, that's great for you. Don't bring anyone else in. I'm glad you reached your goal. But if your goal is to grow, you'll need to partner with the right people.

I want to advise you not to get starry-eyed when looking for a partner (or partners). Many business owners only wait until they can hire the best in the industry. While that reasoning seems logical on paper, it doesn't always translate into a great partnership. You may make yourself ultra-dependent on a person or organization, and if they're really that good, they may see you as a small fish in their big ocean. In other words, they might be your top priority, but you might be at the bottom of their list.

There are two tangible qualities to look for when choosing the right partner(s).

1. Loyalty

2. Hard Work

Everything else can be taught.

Find someone who's excited to be a part of what you're doing, someone who's also passionate about the people you're helping. Find someone who is willing to roll their sleeves up and get into the trenches with you. When you partner with people like that, that creates the foundation for magic to happen.

The good news is it's easier than ever to validate people. If someone were to give you a reference, in less than five minutes you can check that person's website, reviews, LinkedIn profile, Facebook business page, Facebook personal page, etc. When you feel like you've found someone you'd like to enter into some sort of partnership with, have good, honest, meaningful conversations. Make sure that what you need is not just what the other person *agrees* to give, but that what you need is what the other person *wants* to give!

Like every good relationship, some will last forever and others will be short-lived but will create great memories. In other words, some relationships you marry and others you'll date (and hopefully break up with amicably). It's important to know when you've outgrown them and when to move on. That's not to say that you stop working with them. If someone has helped you grow your business to the point that its needs have surpassed what they can deliver, yet they've been loyal and have worked hard, find another position for them. For others, it may be time to move on entirely. Remember to never burn your bridges, though. Smart business-minded folks understand that in business, it's not "Goodbye," it's, "We'll collaborate later."

I Can't Feed My Kids Equity-Flakes

One way many people get into business ownership is by buying their way in or acquiring equity in some way. This can be great—or disastrous. On one hand, Sam doesn't have any money to invest but has passion and skill as a web designer. He's tired of working for people who don't appreciate him, but he doesn't know how or have the money to start a business. Joey D. has a web design business, but he doesn't make enough money to pay Sam what he deserves, yet he sees that Sam can help build the business. Sam and Joey D. come to an agreement: Joey D. will pay Sam less than minimum wage and Sam will work full-time for six months, putting in sweat equity. After the six months, Sam will own twenty percent of the company and will be paid twenty percent of the company's profits, which Joey D. projects to be $7,000 a month.

Sam ends up working far more than the agreed-upon 40-hour workweek. When he complains or attempts to restructure, Joey D. reminds him that he is an owner and that that's what owners do.

After six months, which forced Sam to move back in with his parents, the company is not doing well, and all Sam can make is $2,000 a month—if he's lucky.

I want to caution you about working for someone for a long-term payoff in the form of equity. The sad truth is that more than

80% of businesses fail in the first five years. If someone approaches you with a part-ownership deal, don't jump at it. Nothing is guaranteed except that you're going to give the other person your blood, sweat and tears in the form of your ideas, energy, time, and skill, and you could very well end up with nothing. You and your kids can't get full on equity flakes.

There has to be a revenue plan. If two people start a business 50/50 and they both burn the midnight oil and sacrifice, that's great. But when someone is being brought onto a train that's already moving, you need a plan in the form of a contract. The bad news is you could end up working for free, the business tanks, and you wind up with nothing—or—you could work for free, the company blows up, and you still wind up with nothing. I've been around business folks long enough to know this truth: money can change people.

My advice to you is this: if you have a second source of income, maybe a working spouse, and you feel strongly about putting in sweat equity to help a struggling business in order to get paid with more money and equity down the road, it might be a good idea, provided your spouse agrees. However, if you're the breadwinner and the one who has to pay the bills and put food on the table, run away—fast. If you do decide to do it anyway, protect yourself with a contract. Handshake negotiations have a funny way of becoming one-sided for the person holding the money.

Contracts don't leave room for interpretation. There's no, "But you said this," or, "That's why I said that. Remember?"

Grey areas or unanswered questions can destroy relationships. Contracts are needed because there's so much still unknown. Another big reason for a contract is that while you're working on the agreement, topics that have yet to be discussed or agreed upon get uncovered.

Profits

The first rule of being a good steward with your company's money is this: *it's not your money*. It's the company's money. Too many business owners see the balance in the business bank account as if it's *their* money. They use the company credit/debit card to make personal purchases—Amazon, groceries, tickets to a show, or a pack of gum, and wonder why they don't have money to invest in an important ad spend or to pay their employees. If you blur the line between your money and the company's money, both will suffer.

This is why a bookkeeping service is one of the first things I coach people on purchasing. Give your bookkeeper input on where and when to spend the company's money. Here's where many business owners go wrong and why they end up crashing and burning. They actually think it's their money because it's their business and the bookkeeper doesn't know what he or she is talking about. Joey D, you know web designs because you do it all day, but your bookkeeper knows how to handle money because that's what *she* does all day.

If you're in the Baby Phase, the basic rule of thumb is to figure out how much money you can afford to live on and give yourself a salary. If done in proportion to what the company is making, that will result in always having money in the account. Once you get to the Teenage Phase, raise your salary. Maybe in your Baby Phase you were single and renting a one-bedroom apartment, but now that you've grown your business to the teenage phase, you're married with two kids, paying on a mortgage and two car payments—so you give yourself a raise commensurate with the status of the company and your needs.

It all goes back to your idea of success. You might be in the Baby Phase in your business and already have a spouse and home and car payments. The real question is, how much money do you need to make? If your company brings in $240K a year and you're making $120K a year, and your idea of success is to make six figures—you're good! Congratulations. All you need to do is maintain momentum, which is easier than manifesting it. But if your idea is to have a million-dollar business and one day become a millionaire, take a salary of what you can live on ($30-60K) and invest the rest into the company.

The biggest misnomer about profits is that it's money to spend. If, in your budget, you've factored in how much money to put back into the company with the expenses, then yes—spend away, if that's what you want to do. But if you don't have the amount of dollars set up to invest in the company, the profits you see aren't all profits.

Debt

When you first started your company, you were most likely bombarded with emails and real mail from institutions pre-approving you for a business credit card. People who aren't fiscally trained (which is most people) think, *This is amazing! Free money!* One of the biggest things you *don't* need early on is debt. However, there's a right way and a wrong way to leverage debt.

The Wrong Way: You want to have a booth at the annual widgets convention. With the cost of the flight, hourly wages, hotel, expenses, the booth, and marketing materials, you figure you'll sell 30,000 widgets. So, you take out a $45,000 loan. The convention doesn't go as planned, and now you're in debt.

The Right way: You get an order for 30,000 widgets. Your cost per widget is $1. You sell the widget for $5. Once all of the overhead and other expenses are calculated, you make $3 per widget. Get a $30,000 loan, fulfill your order, and immediately pay the loan back.

The Rule: Use a loan on what *will* make you money, not on what *might* make you money.

Whatever you do, don't get into *any* debt before getting some sort of social proof that your idea will work. Don't mortgage your house on an idea. Through social media, you can engage with people, start a group, join groups, and attend online trainings. In a short amount of time (just a few weeks), you should have some data that there's a market for what you want to do, that you are the person who can do it, and the price point is going to be able to support your financial aspirations.

Today, most businesses can start debt-free. All you need is a Facebook page! You don't need to get into a lease for a fancy office, you can attend meetings at a coffee shop (or via online meeting platforms, such as Zoom or Skype). You don't need a dedicated phone line, an expensive website, or a company car. You don't need to advertise on television, or a thousand other things. Just bring your passion and the capacity to sell and deliver. Leave the debt for those whose company you acquire on the cheap later on.

Don't go into debt for "what ifs." Reality rarely matches our expectations, let alone our hopes and dreams. I compare the lure of a loan to the ocean. It's beautiful to look at, but you can get into a lot of trouble if you don't know how to swim. Even if you're a great swimmer, the riptide can kill you sometimes, or the sharks, or you could drift too far out and drown.

CHAPTER 7

MO MONEY, MO PROBLEMS

Work–Life Balance

It was 2007, and my fiancée and I were in the midst of planning our wedding. Wow, what a chaotic time. The invitation list, the food, the venue, the priest, the DJ, the apartment, the honeymoon, the savings, the wedding gown—it was a hectic, but exciting time. It was certainly not the time to start a business. *Maybe after the wedding.*

We got married and went through the major transition of living with someone for the first time, learning who they really were, having laughs, having fights, cooking at home, cleaning, finding time for friends and hobbies—the first year of marriage is certainly not the time to start a business. *Maybe once we've found our groove,* I reasoned, *I'll invest more time and energy into starting a business.*

Around nine months after the wedding, we had our first baby. (Oh, my god, I can't stop looking at him, he's perfect!) That brought about the diaper changes, late-night cuddles so he could go back to sleep, baby-proofing the apartment, doctor check-ups, feedings, and wanting to hold him. I thought, *maybe once we get used to this parenting thing, I'll dive into starting a business.*

Fast-forward to today: I've been married for over a decade, we own two homes, we have four kids, and I'm working on several businesses. Here's what I learned: the perfect time never showed up. The skies never opened up as a sign that the perfect time had arrived. In fact, there's no perfect time to do anything. There's no perfect time to get married, no perfect time to have kids, no perfect time to buy a home, no perfect time to go on a vacation, and no perfect time to start a business. When I reference the perfect time, I mean *perfect*, where no one would disagree or bring up a contrary point. The perfect time doesn't exist, but that doesn't mean you keep waiting. What it means is that you go for it anyway.

We keep waiting for this concept of balancing out the right amount of time at work with the right amount of time at home. But that's like the common cold; it affects everyone, but no one has found a cure. So, here's what you do: you stop trying to achieve the perfect work-life balance and go with work-life *acceptance*. *Accept* the fact that sometimes you're going to spend more time at work than you expected and sometimes your home life is going to take more time than you expected.

Any major life decision involves some sort of sacrifice, whether it be a sacrifice of time, money, emotions, relationships, energy, etc. Some so-called experts have banged the drum shouting about being willing to put it all on the line. It's almost as if nothing in your life should matter except your business. That couldn't be further from the truth. Without the important people in our lives, we lose our *why.* You just have to come to grips with the fact that there will be times when you won't be able to be home—or at work—when you want to.

Just because there's no perfect or consistent work-life balance doesn't mean there's no work-around. Let me explain: You might have to miss your son's 4 PM baseball game because of a big proposal you need to work on, or you might have to meet an important prospect or take out a big client. That doesn't mean you've sacrificed time with your son for the entire day. When you get home, ask him about his game and be present and actually listen to him. Once that deal comes through, you can ease the guilt of missing his baseball game to close a big deal by taking him to a Yankees game.

I very often try to spend time with my three sons that we call "guy time palooza" where we go on crazy trips out of town, on fishing trips, or have a staycation and visit local area attractions. The point is that my kids know that the hard work I put in and the funding of guy time palooza go hand-in-hand—they're connected.

My wife is supportive of the time I need to put into work, but she also supports guy time palooza. We're all on the same page, so it works. That doesn't mean that missing the baseball game, dance recital, or awards ceremony hurts less, but we all know the reward that's coming. The important thing is to be 100% present when you're at work, whether it's in a team meeting, being with a client, or making calls, and it means being 100% present when you're at home, whether it's listening to your spouse's day, putting the kids to bed, or taking the family out for ice cream. Whatever you're doing: be present.

The good news is that we all deal with people. So, it's totally acceptable to tell your client during the evening meal where you verbally closed the deal that you'll send the paperwork mid-morning because when you get home, you're going to ask your son about his baseball game. Honesty and integrity to yourself are where you win, not in chasing an invisible, perfect balance. That, to me, is a level of success.

I Don't Want to Be a Millionaire

So, what does success mean to you? Close your eyes and envision yourself being successful. What does that image contain? Are you in a house in the woods or in a penthouse suite on Miami Beach? What are you driving? Where do you vacation? You have to be purposeful in your goal. If your goal is that you want to make more money, someone can hand you $5, and you'll have hit your goal.

Most people's comment on success is, "I want to be a millionaire." That's so common that there was even a hit game show about it. To be honest, I don't want to be a millionaire; at least, that's not my goal. In fact, I'd rather be a "dollar-naire." My goal isn't a set amount of cash in the bank. I'm in it for the time freedom. I know some millionaires who are so tied to their jobs that they don't have the freedom to do many of the things they can afford.

If your goal is a Lamborghini, and you get it... what's next? I'm Italian, from the top of my head to the bottom of my feet. When I was a kid, my father's goal was to get a Cadillac. We would all daydream about the family packing into a Caddy and having people look at us as if we were movie stars. It was a great fantasy. Then my father bought a Cadillac. It was beautiful. We stared at it for hours.

As an adult, my dream car was a Cadillac Escalade. I spent hours looking at in online. Whenever someone drove past me with one, I would snap my neck and do a double take. I really wanted that car. Through my business dealings, things went incredibly well for me financially to the point where it made sense financially, for the family and for me, to buy my dream car. I remember going to the dealer; I was so excited. I knew I was going to haggle for the best price, but I also knew that no matter what, I was going to get that car. After some decent negotiations on my end, we settled on a number and I bought my Cadillac Escalade! Driving home to pick up the family in that car is still one of the most cherished and memorable drives of my life. It was literally one of the best feelings in the world for me.

A few weeks later, after the euphoria dissipated, I got into a funk. I wasn't excited about anything. It was as if my joy had been sapped. I wondered how that could be. I'd reached my goal. Just like my dad bought his Caddy, I got mine. I should've been happy. Then I realized the problem: I no longer had a goal. The Lambo or Ferrari didn't excite me. I got complacent. I stopped working as hard. That car didn't excite me long-term like I thought it would. That's when I learned the lesson on goal setting. Goals shouldn't be based on material possessions but on a lifestyle. Not a jet-setting lifestyle, but a life of freedom.

This is why it's said that God doesn't answer all your prayers. They also say, if you want to make God laugh, make a plan.

Some might see that as a curse, but it's not. What *they* know is that when someone meets all their goals and dreams, they don't have anything left to chase after and they become unproductive, complacent, and unhappy.

That's why being a "dollar-naire" suits me just fine. I first heard that term from my economics professor in college. A "dollar-naire" is someone who has enough dollars to pay the bills and purchase whatever else is needed. Being a millionaire is too vague for me. I know plenty of millionaires, and the truth is that more than half of them are in debt! The other half aren't in debt and know that money isn't the goal, it's the scoreboard. My goal is freedom—no debt. I want to pay for what I need and not owe anyone or any institution anything. So, to me, freedom includes being debt-free. My father very often would tell me that most people set a goal of being rich, but they should set the goal of being broke—that means no debt. Then, once you're broke, you can go to work on being rich!

There's a great book I recommend for any parent called, *The Family Board Meeting*, by Jim Sheils. He emphasizes how we only have eighteen summers with each child. Because of my freedom goal, I'm able to make sure that the eighteen summers I have with my kids are spent with them. I'm not worried about building a legacy for the future as much as I'm worried about *living* a legacy *now* with my family, friends, and clients.

CHAPTER 8

MARKETING VS AN ART PROJECT

The Most Important Question

The most important question in having a successful business is the same as it is in sports, as it is in a relationship, as it is in just about everything: what is it that makes you win?

The reason why so many people struggle, even though we all set out to answer that one question, is that the answer is multifaceted. Just like a great-tasting soup is made up of a lot of ingredients with some used more than others, and just as music sounds so amazing coming from an orchestra with some notes played louder than others, there is more than one answer and there are variations within each answer. Don't be disheartened, though. I have a multifaceted answer, complete with variations, that leaves it up to you to see what works best for your product or service, time or availability, finances, skillset, and desire.

Up until this point in the book, we've talked about money, partnerships, profits, investments, and many other things, but that was all to get us on the same page for what I *really* want to teach you in the remaining chapters of this book: How to put it all together so that *you win*.

Unfortunately, many entrepreneurs operate in a "Fire! Ready! Aim!" mentality. Motivation or inspiration hits us and we're on the move before making sure of where we're going or how we're going to get there. Because most entrepreneurs are one-person companies, we feel we can't afford to be idle and have to figure everything out for ourselves as we go along.

This is why we've spent countless hours (which I call the "Hustle Hours") watching YouTube videos on marketing, building websites, sales, or managing finances. It often starts after dinner while the family is having "family time" and it runs into when it's time to put the kids to bed (if you have any) and continues past that to after your spouse goes to bed (if you have one) until late into the night, only to wake up early the next morning. We don't yet have the funds to hire a marketing agency, an accountant, or an assistant, so we do it all ourselves.

In our haste to become successful, we yell from our ramparts, "Fire! Ready! Aim!" and let loose our marketing efforts on the world only to not hit anyone. You have to understand the huge chasm between marketing efforts and a *strategic marketing plan*.

Allow me to shed some light on the current marketing landscape so you can take away something tangible from this book right here and right now.

Marketing in the 2020s

What do you think of when someone mentions marketing? Facebook pages or ads? Google My Business? Business cards? Bus stop advertisements? Television commercials? Billboards? Each one is effective, depending on how it's used. To have a television commercial run regionally won't work as well on the History Channel as it will on Hulu. But most entrepreneurs don't have the funds to do a television commercial, so what do we do? We get a website.

Websites

I've seen some so-called gurus say that you don't need a website. Wrong. You do. Although trends are slowly shifting, most people look up businesses by their websites. In the minds of most people, if you're website doesn't exist, then your business doesn't exist.

For the new business owner, there are three options for building and maintaining your website:

1. **The Do It Yourself-er (DIY)**

These entrepreneurs have some technical skills and figure they should just build their own website instead of paying someone to do what they can figure out. They often know people who built their own websites, so they set out to create theirs.

They'll watch tutorials and work from 10 PM to 2 AM for a week, and *voila*, they have a website! Some do a great job. Some do awful jobs; but either way, it goes up as the #1 representation of them and their company, not realizing that they will be judged by the content, the look, the functionality, and how it all translates to a mobile device, i.e., cellphone. They have a website, but the important question is this: Does the website attract clients or prospects to your business?

2. "I Know A Guy"

We all know someone's nephew or cousin or sister's former college roommate who says they know how to build a website. They jump on the Friends & Family discount or the "Because I'm going to put it on my portfolio, I won't charge you full price" discount, and they're off and running.

Most often, the website comes out better than they could ever have done on their own and without them spending hours on it. The main problem arises if they don't really like the first iteration of it and want some changes made, but the person doing it doesn't really want to address those because they did the work on the cheap, and revisions and updates can get a little more costly or frustrating. But they have a website. Again, the question is: Does this website attract clients or prospects to your business?

3. **The Investor**

   These people hire a marketing agency or website building company and let the pros do the work. They'll get quotes ranging from $1,000 to $30,000 depending on what they want and settle on the best value they can get for what they can afford. They tend to end up with a great looking website done at the estimated time of completion. They have a great looking website, but the question is: Does this website attract clients or prospects to your business?

Again, let me reiterate, you need a website. When we inquire about a product or service on a search engine, their bots and algorithms relentlessly seek them out. It's the modern-day business card. The most important thing about websites isn't the catchy domain name or whether it has video or not, it's whether the website attracts clients or prospects to your business.

If you have a website that isn't eliciting inquiries from clients or prospects, you don't have a website. You have an online art project. If, after a few months, you're not getting traction from your website, you need to do some tweaking or maybe a complete overhaul. And maybe this time, pay more attention to the site's messaging.

Messaging

When I coach business owners, I start with messaging before getting into any form of marketing. In this book, though, I'm mentioning messaging after websites on purpose because that's how most entrepreneurs work, and I don't want to go against the grain on how you most likely operate. Besides, you probably have a website already, so now let's talk about messaging.

Alicia Laszewski, one of my business partners, is an expert at creating the right message for our clients. She utilizes what she calls a Message Map and constructs the pillars of a brand, which become the foundation of everything they project. She then finds various ways to support the core message in order to deliver concise and tantalizing messaging consistently.

The Message Map solves the problem many entrepreneurs face. As business owners, it answers the question we're asked most, and very often, it's the one question we answer incorrectly:

The Question: What do you do?

Seems simple enough, right? Who better than you to answer what it is you do?

Millions of entrepreneurs answer this question wrong and the two biggest ways they do that is by under-explaining: "*I'm a photographer,*" and over-explaining: "*As a kid, my mother said I had a good eye for scenery, although I never believed it. And then one day, my Uncle Jack told me the same thing. Now, mind you, I was studying to be an accountant at the time, so I didn't think anything of it. I graduated with a degree in finance, but found I was unfulfilled...* blah - blah - blah"

Proper messaging should convey what it is that you do, but that's not all. It should also embed a *call to action*, meaning that your response should seamlessly prompt more conversation about what you do.

The photographer could say, "I capture timeless moments in beautiful photographs that hang on people's walls for the rest of their lives."

I don't care if you're selling pizza or planes, jam or jets, you need a clear and concise message because that's what wins every time.

Think of the biggest brands out there. Do you know their message?

Nike – Just Do It

Apple – Think Different

McDonald's – I'm Loving It

When you hear their company names or see their logos, their messages enter your subconscious and you're more apt to purchase from them.

When it comes to messaging, remember this: if you're not telling your story, then someone else is telling it for you. Not only will they tell people what you do, they'll also tell them how you do it, and if you're any good at it. Often, that *someone else* is your competitors.

Networking

I find it sad that most people don't consider networking a form of marketing. Sadly, those are companies that have a tough time growing. I'm going to write this as clearly as I can: if you're an entrepreneur/small business owner, you need to be networking.

Mind you, post COVID-19 Pandemic, the face of networking might change a little, but at the end of the day, nothing beats human interaction. Find what networking events are available to you in your area and attend them. Whether you go to a weekly breakfast or lunch meeting, such as at BNI or a monthly luncheon meeting at your local Chamber of Commerce, you need to let people see you so you can tell them your message.

If you cultivate the right answer to the question: What do you do? You'll give yourself the best chance of turning people you've just met (strangers) into acquaintances (friends) or clients (paying friends).

I use a few of them. My short and sweet answer to what I do is: I'm an outsourced COO. It most often opens the door for a follow up question from whoever asked the first question. "What does that mean?" Aha! The person just focused on me, probably for the first time, and now we're in a conversation. "I help businesses organize themselves through marketing, sales, and strategic implementation in order to grow their business." From there, I can give a quick testimonial or pivot into asking them what they do.

The point is, once you start to utilize a concise message that prompts conversation, you're going to turn into a fantastic networker.

Make sure when you go out to network, that you're networking, not socializing. There's a big difference. People who go out to socialize usually stick to talking to a few people that they come to feel comfortable with, even if they aren't ideal clients. Networkers have a goal in mind and a call to action for people they meet. The call to action could be that they follow you on Instagram or give you their card. The important thing is for you to create a strategy based on your strengths and personality and then execute that strategy.

They key thing about networking is not to be afraid to ask for a referral. "Would you know anyone I may be able to help?" The word *no* pays you the same amount as not asking, but *yes* pays a lot more!

The thing about networking is that it's founded on a *you scratch my back, I'll scratch yours* kind of expectation. Don't be greedy. Don't just look for others to help you. If you're willing to give referrals, you'll most likely get more referrals. Don't forget, if you're just socializing and not getting referrals, you're not networking. You're in a fraternity.

Social Media

At the time of this writing, the major social media platforms are Facebook, Instagram, Twitter, YouTube, and now TikTok is coming on strong. If you're reading this years from now, one or more of these might have gone the way of MySpace, which once was extremely popular but is pretty much just a memory now. While MySpace is gone (Bye, Tom!), the principles of marketing on social media are still here.

"Mike, if I can only use one platform, which one should I choose?" Whether I'm speaking at a National Convention in front of thousands or at a local Chamber meeting of 30-or-so entrepreneurs, that's the question I'm most asked. The answers are the same:

1. Which platform are your clients on?
2. Which platform can you be consistent on?
3. All of them.

Answer number 3 may look contradictory, but the name of the marketing game is the more places you can be seen, the more people will see you. Grant Cardone says it well when he says, and I'm paraphrasing here, *The most successful aren't always the best, they're the most visible!*

When it comes to marketing on social media, don't get too excited about the *Likes* or *Views*, or even the *comments* if they're from people who aren't prospects. Also, don't hold on to posts or videos just because they're not perfect. *Done* beats *Perfect* every time, because Perfect never gets Done. Base everything on whatever helps you best build relationships.

At the end of the day, we do business with people we feel we know, like, and can trust. You may have heard that before, but do you want to know why people keep repeating it? Because it's true! But that doesn't happen from one post or a cool image. It happens through back-and-forth interaction, meaning you have to take time to *like* your followers' posts and reply to comments. *Engagement* is the key to social media success.

I'm going to make this quite simple for you. Here are the two biggest things you need to do to have any success marketing on social media:

1. Know your messaging
2. Be consistent

If you consistently put out good content, you'll be on your way to having substantial conversations with your target prospects.

Podcasts

I was a teacher in the early 2000s and podcasting had just become a thing. I'll never forget attending a workshop on how to use a podcast to teach students. I was blown away by the simplicity and effectiveness of it. I quickly implemented what I had learned by creating a weekly podcast for my class. In it, I let my students know about upcoming assignments for the week, due dates, exams coming up, and a few other things. It liberated me in the sense that I had more time to teach because I no longer had to repeat those daily or weekly reminders; they were in my podcast! I had more instruction time, which gave me a better quality of life because that's what I love to do.

Fast-forward more than a decade and podcasting has climbed out of its niche beginnings and hit the mainstream. I'm still a big fan of the podcast. If you're a business owner who wants to be known as a business leader, I believe the best way to go is to write a book about what you do and have a podcast. Those things will do more to prove that you're an SME (Subject Matter Expert) than anything else.

Just as it did for me as a teacher, it can save you time and consistently give out information you'd like people to know. Everything can be transmitted through a podcast. In fact, one of your CTA's (Calls to Action) can be to send people to listen to your podcast. If someone were to ask you what you do, you could give him or her a short answer and say, "I'd love for you to check out my podcast. Some of the early episodes explain what I do, and I also have some great guests who have delivered exceptional content for business owners."

What separates podcasting from other social media platforms is that you're in someone's ear. It's just you and that other person; it's almost like a one-on-one conversation. People often listen to podcasts when they're alone in a car or while working out, and you'll have a much greater share of their attention than when they're on Facebook or Instagram just scrolling through their feed. With a podcast, you have a better chance of capturing their interest and inspiring them to become fans, followers, and/or clients.

Like everything else, when marketing on social media, messaging and consistency are key. I hope you've picked up that the theme of this chapter is messaging and consistency.

Some entrepreneurs can't go to networking events because they work somewhere else full-time, and their business is a side hustle. That doesn't mean you can't or shouldn't start a podcast. Record it at home and put your message consistently out to the marketplace.

Don't overthink it. Be like Nike and *Just Do It!* It's not a complicated process. You can buy a decent starter kit for around $65, plug it into your laptop, and start recording. Or you can download a good microphone app for even less money and start recording. Like all the social media platforms, it's free to upload and get your message out there. There are even some platforms, such as Anchor, where all you have to do is upload your podcast to their platform and they'll distribute it to all the other major podcasting platforms.

In terms of length, do what's comfortable for you. If you feel that your listeners would like powerful and motivational 10-minute shows, do that. If you think they'd listen to 45 minutes or an hour of content while you interview someone, do that. The secret is to check into which podcasts get better engagement and then do that. Consistently. Your listeners will show you the direction you should go, but first you need to get on the road.

Video

As a kid, I would watch shows like, *Who's the Boss* and *Growing Pains*, feeling like I knew the characters being portrayed. In a way, I considered the characters on the show my friends because, by way of television, they were in my home.

That's the power of video. It allows you to create a connection with people. You can pull back the curtain, even though you do it strategically, and have people build a relationship with you, even if it's in their own minds.

Each Monday morning, I broadcast a *Live* video on one of the social media platforms. Before I start talking, I do a little dance. I do that for two reasons:

1. To be different
2. To connect with people without even talking.

I certainly don't do it because I'm a good dancer or that I like to dance. Disclaimer: I'm not a good dancer. I don't dance at parties or weddings. I'm the guy who sits with other rhythmically challenged guys while my wife dances all over the floor with her friends. Yet, I'm often mistaken for a dancer. Why? Because I've done it consistently.

When it comes to shooting video, in terms of production, quality is important. Lighting, background, and audio are the top three things to focus on. But don't get overly consumed with those things. At the end of the day, people don't care so much about post-production, they're more interested in who you are and whether you have something they want in terms of content or entertainment.

The end goal for video should be the same with how you leverage every other marketing platform: to elicit conversation with qualified prospects. Remember, it's not about you; it's about the people who need your product or service. I certainly don't dance because I think I look smooth doing it. I do it to start a conversation so that I can help more people. I've had people comment on my dancing at conferences, networking events, and many other places. One time, someone came up to me while shopping for groceries at a supermarket, "Hey, you're the one that dances on social media, right?

"Why, yes—yes, I am." I say, smiling and extending a handshake. "And you are?"

Conversation and connection, just as I strategically planned. Again, the key to leveraging social media is NOT about having the best graphics, the coolest videos, the most expensive sets and equipment, or the best outfits. First, understand what it is you do and the proper way to convey that to the world: that's your message. Second, try everything and test to see which things work better and do that over and over again—that's consistency. If you haven't been marketing on social media that way, then you haven't been doing it right. But I have good news for you: you can start all over in a new direction tomorrow!

CHAPTER 9

SALES

Every business, regardless of whether it's a brick-and-mortar store, an online store, business coaching, a service-oriented business, or any other business out there, needs one thing in order to survive. Without this one thing, even if it's funded extremely well, it's not going to survive. That one thing? Sales.

The ability to convince someone that the service or product you're selling—sales—is a love/hate relationship for most people. Sales positions tend to have the highest earning potential, yet most people won't venture into it. As a society, we've been ingrained that in some way, shape, or form, the business of sales is sleazy or dishonest. The image of an in-it-for-himself, willing-to-lie-to-get-the-deal used car salesperson involuntarily pops into our heads.

We walk into a furniture store and we instantly distrust the smiling person who welcomes us in. However, regardless of how most people feel about salespeople, the art of the sale is the thing you depend on most and is the very backbone of our economy.

I'm here to tell you, the business of sales doesn't have to be sleazy, dishonest, or something to hate. When done right, it's a whole lot of fun.

My first sales job was easy; I was great at it. Well, the truth is, I was selling something for free! I worked at an electronics store and gave people a free phone if they signed up for a 12-month service contract. It was commission-based, and like I said, I did well at it. So well, in fact, that I got promoted to the Big Show, selling computers.

I struggled at first. After all, selling a product that costs thousands of dollars is much more difficult than giving away a free phone. I was starting to hate going to work because I wasn't being effective or even useful, and I started to question whether I was made for sales. After considering the prospects of finding a new job, I decided to give it one more shot.

As I've mentioned before, I'm an educator at heart as most of my professional experience dictates, and it didn't take me long to figure out what I was doing wrong. I was trying to sell and not trying to educate. I started learning what the prospect wanted, educating him or her on the different computers we had, and how they could help. Then I left it up to them to choose whether they bought or not. Because of my honesty and helpfulness, many more chose to buy than not.

When I started talking to prospects with the intention of teaching them about the computers and how to best use them, my closing ratio jumped off the charts. I was amazed at some of the things I thought were common knowledge that my prospects had never heard. Not only did my sales skyrocket, but more importantly for me, I started to love going to work again. I felt needed and appreciated because I stopped selling and I started *helping*.

Some of the best salespeople I've hired over the years have a teaching background. It's not that I *require* it, but I do like to know that my salespeople can intelligently deliver a value proposition with integrity and transparency. One thing about teaching: teachers know more than you do about what they're teaching. Teachers are respected. Teachers are valued. Because of that, teachers are valuable.

Full transparency, although I've had great success as a salesperson and I like it, that's not where I hang my hat. My *expertise*, if you will, centers on business growth, strategic planning, implementation, and training. So, I'm not going to spend a lot of time teaching on every aspect of sales. The truth of the matter is there are so many successful sales techniques that if I were to write all I know about sales, I'd have to write an entire book on it, and that's not this book.

When it comes to selling your product or service, I'm challenging you to flip the script: don't think about how to sell your product or service. Instead, focus on enlightening people on it and explaining how it's of value.

As I mentioned before, there are many different techniques in sales, and most of them work well if it suits the salesperson's personality. But out of the myriad of sales techniques, most of them are based on three easy to implement fundamentals.

Here are the three fundamentals in sales:

1. **Ask Questions**

Inexperienced or pushy salespeople go into the sales conversation wanting to *tell*:

"Let me tell you why this product is so great..."

"Check out what it can do for you..."

"This is my resume and why you should trust me..."

Now, there are 8 billion people on the planet, so this works sometimes. However, your odds will increase dramatically if you switch from wanting to tell to wanting to *know*:

"I'm happy you contacted me. Can I ask what you're looking for?"

"What's the current state of your business/health/relationship/sales (Add what your product or service helps with here)?

As human beings, we want to know that we are listened to and understood. If you—the salesperson—don't let us know that you understand our problems because you've listened to us, you've created a roadblock to completing a sale.

Now, you may know my problem better than I do because you've been selling your service for a long time and you might even be better at explaining my problems better than I am, but if I didn't even have an opportunity to express it to you, whether in person or over the phone, I'm not going to trust that you do. And if I don't trust that you're trying to help me, then I'm going to be thinking that you're trying to sell me. While I love to buy; I hate to be sold.

Here's a healthy barometer to find out if you're asking enough questions (or the right questions). If you're doing more than 30% of the talking in the first few minutes, you're not doing it right.

It's common knowledge that we do business with people we feel we know, like, and trust. By asking the right questions, you're gaining trust.

The right questions are open-ended questions. Closed-ended questions feel as if you're trying to herd your prospect through a maze of carefully crafted questions.

Closed-ended questions are answered by a yes or no, or just a few words.

Is this your first time here?

What's your favorite color?

Do you go to the beach often?

How long have you worn glasses?

Open-ended questions are answered by an explanation.

Tell me about the book you want to publish. Why is it important to you?

What is the biggest challenge in your business right now?

How can I bring value to you or your business?

What questions can I answer for you today that can help you better understand the process?

Tell me about the outcome you're trying to achieve. What does that look like?

Dig deep. Don't just ask the preliminary questions. Get to a personal level: *Why is that important to you?*

The goal isn't to ask enough questions so that you can understand the client's problem. The goal is to ask enough questions for *the client* to know that you understand his or her needs. When implemented correctly, the prospect will then start to ask you questions. That allows you to get to the next step.

2. Storytelling

We are story-driven beings. Ever since we were children, we've been ingrained to either learn or to be educated through stories. Whether it was Bible stories or Disney stories, "Once upon a time..." stories have been with us all our lives. They move us to tears, to cheers—and to purchase.

Once again, we do business with people we feel that we know, like, and can trust. Now that you've established trust by asking the right questions (and enough of them), get them to feel that they know you and like you. Tell them a story that explains the features and benefits, maybe on how it helped others in a similar situation. Don't get confused; if you have a person's undivided attention, someone who is listening to why you're doing what you're doing, you're operating in high sales efficiency.

The best way to get that attention is to tell someone your why. Odds are you're not the first person to do what you're doing and you're probably not the only person doing what you're doing. Your why will help you sell someone that product or service. Your why can help you stand out from the other five salespeople they've talked to, and your why could turn you into a friend. Your why will also keep you motivated when that personal connection is made and they still go to the guy who charges less, and it stings because you left it all on the table.

If you've never written down your why—why you started your business or why you're working at the company you're at, please put this book down and do that now! It'll be here when you're done.

Once you've explained your why and why the prospect should consider buying your product or service, there's just one part left. Fair warning, this is the most difficult part.

3. Ask For the Sale

Another one of my dad's sayings was, "If it were easy, everyone would do it." This statement rings true when it comes to sales. After all, and as I previously mentioned, it's one of the ways to earn the most income. But here is where the rubber meets the road and where sales professionals differentiate themselves from order takers. If you only asked great questions and told a great story, that would only make you a great conversationalist. Great conversationalists don't close tons of deals. Sales professionals do.

What you *don't* want to do is to make someone feel pressured, on the spot, or uncomfortable. The close is expected. Whomever you're talking to about your product or service knows that this is what you do for a living. Being that they have engaged you in conversation, emails, direct messages, or smoke signals, they expect you to ask them whether they're going to buy or not. Don't make it weird. Don't make it mean more than it does. They're not deciding whether they think you're a good person. It's not a personal indictment about you or your product or service. They're either going go buy or they're not. Just ask for the sale.

Now, there are many different ways to ask for the sale. There's not one sure-fire way to close that works on everyone all the time. Here are a few ways I've either used or have been used on me that I've liked:

- Does all of this sound fair (good) to you?
- What would you like us to do next?
- Would you like me to send over the paperwork?
- Is there a particular date you're thinking of starting?
- Let's start to put together a plan to roll this out.

REMEMBER, MONEY IS THE FERTILIZER THAT ALLOWS YOUR BUSINESS TO GROW. IT'S THE GAS IN THE TANK. IT'S THE WATER IN THE FISHBOWL. WITHOUT IT, THE FLOWER, FISH, AND FERRARI DIE.

There will be times when the prospect isn't ready to make the decision. It's not that they're putting you off. They might have to talk to a spouse or first put other things in order before moving forward with you. Do yourself a favor and respect that.

Some sales techniques teach that if someone tells you that they'll get back to you in a week, respond with:

- I'm sorry, I thought I answered all of your questions and you said it looked like a good deal for you.
- What's going to change in a week?

- Did I not answer satisfactorily?
- What are you still hung up on that's keeping you from making the decision now?"

I hate that guy. Don't be that guy. To be fair, those salespeople are taught to get the yes or no. A *no* is not the best answer, but it's an okay answer. Sure, you lost the deal, but at least you know to move on and put your energy and time into someone who might say yes. Being aggressive does work sometimes, but it won't build lifelong customers. There's a better, more strategic way of respecting the person's timeframe while still getting to a yes-or-no answer.

If someone asks you to give him or her a week, try answering with something like this:

"Sure, Mike. I can get back to you in a week. But actually, is a week enough time for you to figure out what you're going to do? Would you rather I call you in 10 days or two weeks?"

By giving the prospect more time than they ask for, you're taking your name and likeness completely out of the sleazy, pushy, will-do-anything-for-a-sale salesperson category. They might answer with, "Thank you, but a week is fine," or "Yes. Two weeks would be great," and that's okay. Once the two weeks are up, you can expect your yes-or-no answer. If you pressure people to make a decision before they're ready, the most common answer you're going to get is that they're still not sure. So, give them enough time and then ask for the sale again.

The Paperwork

If your sale hinges on a contract, make sure it's easy to read. Lawyers who write contracts have a gift for hiding the meaning of the contract in the middle of big, seldom-used words. Make sure your contract is colloquial (there's a big, seldom-used word!), meaning that it's okay if a lawyer drew it up, but make sure that every word is easy to understand. The last thing you want is for your soon-to-be customer to think that you tried to pull a fast one on them and have them sign something different from how you said it would be.

Also, the word *contract* has a binding, no-fun, connotation to it. Many people don't want to sign contracts unless they're professional athletes. I often refer to it as *the paperwork* or *the agreement*.

"I'll send over the paperwork today, and please let me know if it reads anything differently from what I mentioned. If it looks right to you, sign it and send it back, and we can begin. If anything looks off or raises a concern, please call me and I'll resolve it."

I'll end this chapter on sales with these helpful reminders:

1. It's not personal. It's a game.
2. The other person is expecting it.
3. Ask questions, tell stories, and ask for the sale.
4. If you don't get an answer right then, find out when the prospect will know, then give him or her even more time than they ask for.

5. Send an easy-to-read contract (which you'll call, "the paperwork" or "the agreement," and offer to clarify anything that looks incorrect.

I've read many books on sales. I've been to many sales conferences. I've listened to many audiobooks and watched videos on sales. Out of the massive sales library that exists, I recommend these three books if you want to get deeper into the psychology of the sale or are looking for a more step-by-step framework to build your sales process on.

Sell or be Sold, by Grant Cardone
Never Split the Difference, by Chris Voss
Fanatical Prospecting, by Jeb Blount

It's important to have a process. If you have a script, know it, but just as importantly, know how to deviate from it when you need to. It's also important, depending on your business and the size of it, to have some sort of a CRM (Customer Relationship Management) system or software. Be sure to make your process duplicatable so your business can grow.

Success doesn't start when you start a business.

Success doesn't start when you make your first sale.

Success doesn't start when you hire your first employee.

Success begins when you start to grow and scale.

That's why my passion is working with businesses that are ready to take on the challenge of growing and scaling, both effectively and efficiently.

CHAPTER 10

NO PEAKS AND VALLEYS

"Every person in their life has had a million-dollar idea. The question is, are you going to take action?" – Sara Blakely Founder of Spanx

Have you heard of Sara Blakely? She's the first self-made billionaire. She still owns 100% of her company, Spanx. Sure, she went to Oprah and her business took off, but do you know the story of her hustle that got her to Oprah?

After years of working as a sales rep, selling fax machines, she was in her car, depressed that her life had settled to where she was. She yelled out, "I'm in the wrong movie! Call the director, we need a rewrite, I was meant to be in another movie!"

She goes on to say that she said to the universe, "I promise, if you give me the idea, I'll take it to the limit to make it successful."

Two years later, she thought of her product and called it Spanx. (For those who don't know her product, it's a lightweight, woman's undergarment, now called Shapewear, that helps women control "trouble areas" and make their silhouette look slim and streamlined).

As those in retail know, products just don't magically appear on store shelves, there's a process to it. Sara's blessing was that she didn't know the process. All she knew was it would be a great fit with the Neiman Marcus stores. So, not knowing any better, and going with who she was, a salesperson, she cold called a Neiman Marcus store. The woman who spoke to her laughed and informed her that they have an entire department that does the purchasing. Sara asked for the number and got it.

She then called the buying department in Dallas. She said, and I'm paraphrasing here, *I have a product that women are going to love and it's going to outsell everything else in the store!*

The buyer replied. "Great. Send over a sample." And was about to get off the phone but Sara knew in her gut that she had to push the product. She asked the woman if she would fly to Dallas if the woman would give her 10 minutes. "If you fly all the way over here, sure, I'll give you 10 minutes."

Sara recounts a funny story about how she wanted to take her lucky red, beat-up backpack. Her friends told her she was crazy. "You're going to Neiman Marcus, buy a Prada bag to put the product in and just return it when you come back!"

When she walked into the buyer's office, she started explaining the products capabilities to the buyer. The woman's non-verbal communication told her she was about to blow the deal. She looked at the woman and said, "Will you come to the bathroom with me?" She took the product out of her lucky beat-up backpack. "You have to see what it does, only then will you get the full power of it."

The woman, dressed to the nines, with everything matching including her fingernails, walked to the bathroom with Sara. In the bathroom, Sara gave the woman a good look at her bottom, under the white jeans she wore. It was obvious that she had some cellulite. Then she went to a stall and put on her Spanx and came out and did a twirl for the woman – smooth and round.

"I get it." The buyer said. "I'll put it in seven stores."

Sara's story doesn't stop there. She called everyone she knew in the seven cities and told them to please buy her product and that she would reimburse them! Then she went to each store, before they opened, and talked to the staff. She gave them away to the female staff members and stayed in the stores to help sell them. Once they sold out, the buyer put them in more stores.

Once Spanx entered into 21 Neiman Marcus stores in California, she made a 21-day trip and visited a store a day, training the staff and helping to sell her product. She gave it all she had, and then that's when Oprah called.

I started this chapter with a quote from Sara Blakely, but now that you know a little of her story, I want you to read it again so you can truly see her meaning.

"Every person in their life has had a million-dollar idea. The question is, are you going to take action?" – Sara Blakely Founder of Spanx

Growing Is the Hard Part

Starting a business is easy. Growing one is the hard part. I see many people say it's all about spending money on marketing and getting your hustle or your grind on. Um, no. There's more to it than that. Much more. Plenty of people have grinded it out on a bad idea or business and failed. Business growth requires strategy.

Businesses are much like the boundaries of countries. Like it or not, everywhere a country ends and another begins, the boundary has been shaped by force (armies, i.e., war.) There will come a point where your business can't grow. It will not be strong enough to take over more market share. Your army, usually an army of one (you), might have great skill at what you do but probably not enough skill in growing a business or creating the right processes or hiring and training the right people.

So, in order to expand their businesses boundaries, many business owners will say yes to anything because they still don't know anything about growing a business—they just want to get business. Forbes.com states that more than 80% of businesses don't make it past year five, and that's one of the major reasons why! Mentalities like, "We'll staff up!—We'll learn as we go!" or the worst of them all, "Fake it 'til you make it!" do not constitute a substantial business model.

All that being said, I'm about to help you get more out of your business than ever before. Are you ready for this? It's comes quick, so don't miss it.

Say *No*

A great mentor once told me to learn to leverage the power in the word *no*. Even though it's only a two-letter word, it's quite possibly the most powerful word in the English language. It's extremely versatile in that it can disappoint, excite, confuse, or define you. I want to teach you how to leverage *no,* so that you can grow your business. You reading this book already tells me that you've invested in your company and future. People like you usually reach certain levels of accomplishment. The more that people get to know, like, and trust you, the more your business will grow, which is wonderful. However, that road has some sharp corners.

As you know, I have four kids. My third son loves to wear my second son's clothes around the house. The problem is that he's swimming in them and he trips and falls when he tries to do the things he enjoys. He doesn't fit in them. Sure, he's wearing clothes and can move around a bit, but he can't do the things he needs to do effectively. Now, on the flip side, when my second son wears the same clothes, he can do everything he needs to do because they fit him, as expected.

Quite often, clients will try to put you in a situation where you don't fit. They'll ask if you can do things for them that aren't exactly in your wheelhouse. In your attempt to please them, you'll bend here and there and stretch here and there, often resulting in you realizing that you can provide a more robust service and make more money in the process. However, the sharp turn comes when you say yes to doing something that you have no business doing. This usually ends badly. Because you're not an expert at something you offered to deliver, the client has a poor experience with you, resulting in that person not hiring you again.

Usually, business owners who just start out are quick to acquiesce to perform services or deliver a product they have no idea how to fulfill. They don't have much business coming in and they say yes to anything. It's important to understand when you start a business that you have no reputation. If you say yes to things you're not good at, you'll quickly get a bad one. If you can say no to things that you're not great at, you'll get a reputation for being honest. When you're honest and authentic, you're on the fast track to success.

To be clear, saying no to an opportunity doesn't mean you have to walk away from the business. You can say, "I'm sorry, Mark. I don't do that, but I can find you someone who's great at it." It's also perfectly fine if you will take on the additional duties for more money, just make sure that it's something you know you can deliver on.

A business owner once proudly told me, "I say yes to everything!"

"Everything?" I asked. His comment seemed a little irresponsible, so I wanted to make sure he wasn't purposefully overexaggerating.

"Yes, Mike. Everything. I say yes to everything, and when the business comes in, I tell my team to figure it out."

As a business owner, you need to know your company's limitations. Can you imagine being an employee in this guy's company? Remember, "I'll figure it out!" is not a strategic plan. Knowing your *no* boundaries will help your business run smoothly, attract the right clients, and gain you more confidence in the marketplace and with your team.

Sometimes, you have to say no to yourself. Many entrepreneurs are quick to purchase an online course or go to YouTube to learn a new skill. Sure, you can learn to build a website, but is it worth a week of your time and attention to do something that isn't going to represent you with quality?

Peaks and Valleys

To be successful, you need to read and ride the correct waves of success. Not all success waves are surf worthy. Bad business or too much business can be detrimental to your company's health. When I worked as a teacher, I made $40K a year, every year. It was sustainable. I got married, bought a house, and had two kids all on that salary. I could depend on the same check every two weeks. I also loved what I did. It would have been easy and sustainable to stay there. But you know that as entrepreneurs, our minds don't work that way.

In my first year of business, I easily made more than six figures, and a few years later, I broke the seven-figure mark at one point. While the money more than doubled in the first year, the income stream was sporadic, at best, in the years that followed. Every day, you're fighting to grow your company, but the inconsistent money coming in hurts you as much as it helps you. You need to leverage the peaks when a lot of money is coming in to help you get through the valleys when little to no money is coming in.

ABC's Wide World of Sports had a great introduction to their program. Legendary announcer, Jim McKay would say, "...the thrill of victory (and show people performing athletic marvels) ... and the agony of defeat (and show a skier and a motorcycle rider wiping out horribly)." There are many thrills in business ownership, but if we go by statistics, most of them end in agony. One of the ways to stay in business is by never thinking you've made it and that you have it all figured out. I liken businesses at times to trees. Every day, your tree needs sunshine and to be watered regularly. However, on any given day, a storm can hit and knock it all down.

Most companies die in the valley when things slow down. True leaders understand that there is more future growth potential in a downturn than when things are running optimally. When you're at full capacity, you can't plan and you can't pivot. But when you're in the valley, you can actually have a better vision of your company's path than when you're peaking.

The valley is where your best work is done. The hot word today is *pivot*. I have to pivot. I'm going to pivot. How can I pivot? Who can help me pivot? Entrepreneurs in the valley quickly look to pivot, to doing something else. While some companies should do that if that's what the market has decided, most companies need to minimize their offerings and get back to the basics. I prefer to *refine* rather than *pivot*.

This planet has more human beings on it than ever before in the history of humankind. There are more than enough people for you to help by refining your skill, your messaging, your production, and your service that will make your business expand. Too many entrepreneurs get scared when things don't go well, so they pivot here and they pivot there. One of the side effects of that is that they never grow as businesspeople. I know a business owner who's been in business for more than 20 years who's pivoted so often that he's always been in start-up mode. He has no idea how to grow his business because every time he encountered the same set of problems, he started over.

In business, we try to pivot or expand into areas where we think we can get into and where we can even get the deal, but maybe we don't fit. You can take the business, but sometimes it pays to find someone to partner with who can complete the tasks that need to be done while you're building up your company. This way, the client is happy, you're happy, and your new partner is happy as well. Congrats, you have now allowed yourself to gain a new client and build a solid reputation for your company.

Don't pivot out of fear. If you ride the same roller coaster all the time, you'll gradually become less afraid of it. Eventually, you learn to anticipate the twists and drops and can master your emotions getting on it. Once you've mastered that coaster, then you can master another with a lot less fear. If you ride different roller coasters all the time, the same fear will grow in your belly and you'll never conquer your fear of roller coasters.

Oh, but we love peaks! Gary Vaynerchuck, better known as Gary V, calls peaks "the clouds" and valleys "the dirt." He mentions how much we love being in the clouds. We like it so much that we stop doing what we did to get there, and well, we faceplant into the dirt—which is where the real work takes place. However, the athletes who are wildly successful, such as the ones who have been dubbed the GOATs (Greatest Of All Time), work harder once they get to the peaks.

Everyone's peak is not the same. Yours might be money. Someone else's might be being able to afford a dream car, while for someone else it could be when they hire a family member. It's important to define *your* peak. Write down what success looks like to you. Understand where you are, where you want to go, and write it down so that when you get there, you can enjoy it. Celebrate your successes. Just don't stop working so that you can have more of them.

I have a tree in my backyard, a crepe myrtle, that only blooms once a year. Each year I told my wife, "If it doesn't bloom, its gone," and she would say, "But, it's so beautiful when it blooms. Give it time." One year it didn't bloom, and I told my wife it was time for it to go. Thinking that its lifespan had culminated, I cut it down and put dirt over the stump. Well, I hadn't taken it out by its roots, so it came back stronger and bigger than ever. It's bloomed every year since. Each time I get down on myself, my wife reminds me about how that tree came back. I gave up on that tree, but my wife didn't give up on it, and the tree didn't give up on itself. The moral of this story is: don't give up. Stay true to what your ultimate view of success is and keep fighting for it.

What's the Goal?

Why did you start a business? What's your end goal? What's your why? Do you even know when you've gotten stale, stagnant, and are becoming irrelevant to the market? Some people's goal is to take their business from $2 million a year to $5 million, but if the owner is still working 80 hours per week, has he really reached his goal?

Are you growing as a business owner? Are your employees growing in their craft? Business goals shouldn't be all about money. I know someone who had a great restaurant. and because he was making hand over fist, he decided to open more. That's what you do, right? No. Not blindly, it's not. Putting the same hamster wheel in another part of town isn't really growth. He went from making $100K a year working one restaurant, to working much harder in two restaurants that paid him an average of $50K a year each. His revenue stayed the same, but his staff, stress, and responsibilities doubled.

It's not all about the dollars in your personal bank account. If you earned $300K last year, would you be more successful if you kept your employee count the same and worked just as hard to make $400K? Or would you be more successful if you made the same $300K, hired two more people, and had more free time to spend with loved ones and travel?

Again, what's your goal? If you don't know it, how will you ever know when you've achieved it? How will you know when to increase it? Take a moment now and write out your goals. It's the only way to get there.

My father always said that the difference between a dream and a goal is that a goal is a dream with a date on it!

CHAPTER 11

IMPLEMENTATION

Congratulations. You've started your business, gotten a lead, had the sales conversation/communication, sent a contract, got it signed, and payment was made! You can exhale. You've made it.

Oh wait. You haven't made it as far as you think. In fact, after everything you've done in marketing and sales to get business, you haven't even started working yet. Everything you did was just so that you can actually *start* working, especially if you have a service-based business. Tighten your belt and roll up your sleeves—it's time for the hardest part; although, if done right, can also be the most fun part—Implementation.

Implementation: The process of putting a decision or plan into effect. *Dictionary.com*

Implementation: When a product or service goes from your business to your customers. *Mike Ficara*

The lifeblood of any business is the sale. Without sales, there's no money. It's similar to a wedding; without a wedding, there's no legal spouse. A sale is much like a wedding, too, in the sense that you put so much work into it. You plan your wedding: who you're going to marry, the date, the location for the wedding and the reception, the budget, the guests, the food, etc. You plan your business in the same way: your value proposition, how much you're going to charge, etc., But after the sale, the work begins, just like after the four-hour wedding extravaganza, the marriage begins.

Just as a marriage is filled with agreements and disagreements, highs and lows, budgetary concerns, time restraints, expansion, etc., the implementation stage also has many facets to it. Promises have been made. Expectations have been established. Assurances that everything will run smoothly, calmly, and confidently have been given. Now, your client is eagerly awaiting that which was sold. If you thought the pressure was in the sale, you're mistaken. The pressure really starts after the sale has been made and it's time to deliver.

Here is what makes or breaks a company. You can have the best marketing strategy executed to perfection, you can be an elite salesperson or have a great sales team, but if you don't deliver, your dream of entrepreneurship will turn into a nightmare.

One of the reasons people start their own business is because they're great sellers or they are great at doing something. They've sold a product or service for someone else and seen how much money they made for someone else, helping that person reach their dream rather than their own. Now, they've struck out on their own, taking with them the same great salesmanship but little experience with the full brunt of the fulfillment. They *assume* that the implementation is easy, maybe because they've seen it up close or they've been a part of it, but they've never done every aspect of it.

So, without having the real-world experience of taking a client from A to Z, they make promises and sell something that either doesn't yet exist (like the way they're going to fulfill the expectation or a product or team members that haven't been tested yet) and ultimately hang their business out to dry. Unfortunately, many people are better at selling something that doesn't exist than delivering what they promise.

During the most recent Tech Boom (late-2000-2010s), I worked with many pre-revenue companies led by passionate and intelligent entrepreneurs with great ideas. During this time, many people were looking to invest in the next big thing! Sure, you had the big VC (Venture Capitalist) firms funding businesses out of Silicon Valley and New York, but I also saw people asking friends and family to put money into their businesses. Many people, after watching the .com explosion make a lot of people rich, didn't want to miss out on investing in the next big app or idea!

We all know the old saying that if you build it, they will come. Many of the conversations I had with a lot of tech entrepreneurs ran in another direction. After a brief conversation I had with one too many clients, I developed a motto for many of them. I would never say it aloud but would think it often: *Once I get the funding, then I'll build it!*

They would ask for money and some of the least fortunate ones would get it, only to later realize that they didn't have the experience to deliver and/or they didn't have a contingency plan for the unexpected things that always happen. After being part of (or a close bystander) to many companies that soared and some that sank, I've come up with four fundamental things that help companies make the best of the investments they've received.

The Four Keys to Delivering:

1. ***Give it Away for Free***

   During my teenage and college years, like many kids at that age, I worked at restaurants. I was actually an integral part, even at that early age, of helping two well-known restaurant companies open new locations in my area. Both of them did what's called a *soft opening*, meaning they invited the employees' friends and family and fed them for free. It wasn't so much that they wanted people to taste their food, it was more to test their systems and processes: to see how well the wait staff serviced the customers, how the food processing system worked, how many incoming orders the cooks could handle before getting really backed up, how well the hostess communicated with patrons who had been waiting for a while, how quickly the bartenders made the drinks, and every other aspect of what it takes for a restaurant to run efficiently so that people come back.

What they lost in costs (the wholesale cost of the food and the employees' hours), they more than made up for by seeing what worked well and what they still needed to fix. The restaurants made the necessary adjustments and, a few weeks later, opened to the general public—paying customers—and provided a great experience to first-time customers who went on to become regular customers. The tactic isn't as much a *give-it-away-free* play, as it is a *give-it-away-free-for-now* play so that you can then sell it to more people.

Maybe you don't have a product you think you can afford to give away for free, and if that's the case, maybe you shouldn't. However, perhaps you can give a heavy discount and let your initial clients know that the reason you're giving it away at such a good price is so that, if they like it, they'll come back or tell others about your product or service.

2. ***Case Studies and Testimonials***

Consumers are getting smarter by the day. Gone are the days when America was young and charlatans would sweep through every city and town to sell a tonic that grows hair to bald people, leaving with bags of coins before people could realize they had been scammed. We have the Better Business Bureau, Yelp, Google, Amazon reviews, and many other ways to verify that what someone is trying to sell us is what they say it is. What we're looking for is validation.

If you don't have any customers, it's nearly impossible to answer these questions in a way that would convince us to buy:

"How does this work?"
"Who else has bought this?"
"How did it work for them?"

Another reason to give something away for free or at a deep discount is to get real-world case studies, meaning real data you can use to sell your product or service to more people. A business coach who can't prove they've ever worked with anyone will have an incredibly difficult time beating another business coach who can prove they worked with a client who wanted a 25% increase in sales in a year but was able to deliver that client a 35% increase in nine months. Case studies and testimonials are incredibly valuable and not just for companies that are just starting out.

Sure, they are important for the sales process, but they're equally important in the implementation process because they help manage expectations. It's a great way to Story Tell the client the journey your service is going to take them through. That way, they can envision themselves working with you and having similar or better results than the people whose case study they're reading.

3. *A Plan and a Process*

Whether you're selling ice cream or managing a million dollars of someone's assets, in order for your company to grow, you need a plan and a process. The lack of a plan and a process is the single biggest reason why people remain working solo in their single-person company rather than actually growing a sustainable business.

Many gifted people can sell and deliver, but that doesn't mean they can run a company. That takes a totally different skill set. If they never learn it, they'll stay grinding for the rest of their lives wondering why, as talented as they may be, they haven't made it big yet.

A plan and a process can duplicate your strengths and provide support for your weaknesses. Imagine hiring someone and, instead of taking time off because you're training the person, handing them a manual, them reading it, and going on to fill in the gaps and not taking nearly as much time in training. The faster you can equip a new person to work independently from you, the quicker you can do other things. Now you won't have to be involved in every aspect of the sale, every customer service conversation, or every fulfillment action, and your business can grow—thrive, even.

For the customer, having a plan and purpose gives them the same great service everyone else receives. It's exhausting to have to treat every client differently. When that's the case, just 4–6 clients can be all you're able to handle. It's impossible to grow that way. People are not all that unique. You can create a plan or process that ensures a suitable experience for people of all walks of life.

The more customers you get, the more data you'll have to optimize the customer experience, making it more likely that you'll get more repeat customers and/or referrals. You can fake it 'til you make it and get on base, but without a plan and process, you'll never hit home runs.

4. ***Customer Service***

Many entrepreneurs undervalue customer service. Maybe they're already overwhelmed with the marketing, sales, and fulfillment so they don't put time into making sure the customer is enjoying the ride. This is a huge mistake.

Good customer service can cover even the biggest screw-ups. Even if you make a huge mistake, if you're customer service is stellar, you can still save the business and increase the relationship.

Here's a pillar that helped people build multi-billion-dollar corporations that has been lost today: *Pick up the phone and call your client!*

We'll call our prospects all day long, but once we convert them to clients, we put them on a cruise control method of thinking and go back to calling more prospects. Nobody can give you better data than current clients. No one.

People will buy from you if they feel they know, like, and can trust you; everyone says that. What people *don't* say is that, once they don't, they'll leave you. Reputation management is an important ingredient for business growth. One of the true marks of success is to have an employee who believes in you and your product or service so much that their passion for the company translates into treating your clients with empathy, professionalism, and wisdom.

Remember this golden rule: When it comes to customer service, Silence is not Golden.

Under-Promise and Over-Deliver

When you sell, sell the realistic expectation, not the unattainable dream. When we over-promise, our clients will get mad at us even if we don't do anything wrong. Their discontent will be based on the fact that we did a good job but not the out-of-this-world job we told them we'd do. However, many people are so intent on getting the sale that they don't realize when they're no longer selling what they can actually deliver and begin to describe a perfect-world scenario that doesn't exist.

You only have one chance to make a good first impression. With many people, you have many chances. You might be able to make a great first impression, but if their latest dealing or interaction with you was bad or underwhelming, they start to create your reputation. So, after your one chance to make a good impression happens, it gets replaced by your reputation. That could be a good thing or not, depending on what you sold and how you delivered. Be careful not to exhaust the first group of people who want to believe in you and provide you the benefit of the doubt. People like that don't come around often.

Unfortunately, bad news travels faster than good news. You can do a great job with someone and they may never thank you. They may think, *Well, that's what I paid him for. It's not like he went out of his way to do me a favor.* That client might be a client for life, but they're still less likely to write up a good review. On the other hand, a person who feels cheated is more likely to write up a bad review. Bad reviews go up quickly and get more engagements than good ones. A bad reputation is like an ugly scar or a stupid tattoo. It's hard to hide and you wish you didn't have it, but it goes with you everywhere. That being said, if you handle your mistakes from a humble place, you can learn some of your greatest lessons and have some good stories to tell.

My advice is this: if there's something you can do extra for the client, don't even tell him or her during the sales process if you don't have to. Get the deal and start to deliver what they expect. Then, at the opportune time, over-deliver. Hit them with that free bonus or extra time.

I get it. When you run your own business, you juggle a lot of balls. It's hard to keep them all up in the air and in the proper rotation. There will be times when you'll have to focus on some things more than others. However, if you can implement what I taught in this chapter, if a ball falls down, it's not going to kill the act. You're doing a great job when you focus on the client. If the client focuses on you, you're in trouble. Sustainability and growth feed off of sales and implementation. Keep your clients the center of your attention and you'll get more and more of them.

CHAPTER 12

"IT MEANS YOUR FUTURE HASN'T BEEN WRITTEN YET. NO ONE'S HAS! YOUR FUTURE IS WHATEVER YOU MAKE IT. SO, MAKE IT A GOOD ONE!"

There's a saying that I agree with but also disagree with at times. Maybe you've heard it: Experience is the best teacher.

In many cases, it's absolutely true. If you fall on your face trying to pop a wheelie on your bike, you'll either learn how to adjust your weight or you'll learn to never do it again. The problem with this saying in business is that although it's true, accruing experience can take a lot of time, years or decades even. To exacerbate the problem, business moves almost as fast as the speed of light these days, and it's only going to move faster. So, while experience is the best teacher, you can still learn from other teachers. Meaning, as you wrap up on reading this book, you can learn from my experience and start ahead. Why start at level 1 or 2 when you can jump to level 10?

There is no blueprint for being successful. Most people think business success is like following a map, or as it would be said in today's time, a GPS. They think if they do A, B, and C, they will automatically get to E, F, and G. However, almost no one gets to his or her desired destination at the time the GPS predicts. The ETA (Estimated Time of Arrival) is rarely ever met. A GPS can't account for rain, traffic, car accidents, bathroom breaks, flat tires, running out of gas, or stopping for food. You'll ultimately get to where you want to be if you stick to it, but not everything in business goes according to plan. Remember, what works for you may not work for someone else.

I'd also like to challenge the notion that only those who are *there* can help get you *there*. While I give credence to that, it's not an absolute truth. If you're going to hire someone to coach you, then yes. Get a coach who has been to where you want to get to. But to say that person is the only one that can help you is false. The truth is, if you're open to learning, you can learn something from anyone. It doesn't take an expert to see our blind spots. I've read many great books on business and mindset, I've taken many courses, and I still do because I learn from them. But I'm still open to learn from anyone. If you limit who can teach you, you'll limit what you can learn.

Great CEOs treat janitors with the same respect as executives. First, it's a matter of decency and integrity, but they also know that the person wiping the floor could share something about his homelife or they could talk about a sporting event that could shift the way the CEO thinks on a business-related issue or a relationship-related issue. The CEO knows that the janitor knows things he or she doesn't know. The janitor knows how to fix a leaky pipe; he's got a process. He starts off by putting the Wet Floor sign and then goes to the next step. A CEO can take from that and learn to put other's first, like his employees, over the shareholders.

I've had, and always will have, mentors from all walks of life. I've seen money inflate egos and the same people who would talk to a certain person suddenly finds himself too important. When I was teaching, another teacher taught me a valuable lesson. His classroom was down the hall from mine. He hated teaching. He was burned out. His neglecting to teach or invest in his students caused them to not respect him as they did other teachers. Without him saying anything to me, he taught me to get out of teaching well before I got burned out and didn't want to teach anymore. It was a valuable lesson. Another time I worked for a woman who owned a highly successful company. Even with all of her success, she was short-tempered and mean-spirited. Without knowing it, she taught me what not to do once I became a boss.

In summation of this book, I trust I've shared with you solid, tangible things you can implement right away and you have filed away things you can do for your company once it grows a little more. There is a lot to take in when growing a business: the process, marketing, sales, and implementation – they are all necessary but all of them are not equally important at the same time all of the time. Balance is not everything being 50/50. Balance is having the wherewithal and foresight to know when to work more on a particular part of the company so that the ship stays afloat and going in the right direction.

Wax On, Wax Off.

One of my favorite movies as a kid was The Karate Kid. The story of Daniel and Mr. Miyagi always resonated with me. Daniel was in a new environment. He felt lost and out of place. To make things worse, he was being bullied—like many people who decide to start a business and get bullied by marketers, competition, and the market. Then he met Mr. Miyagi who, to me, set the standard for mentors. If you've seen the movie you know how this went down. Daniel, (called Daniel-san by Mr. Miyagi) is told to do seemingly menial tasks. All he wanted to do was learn karate but his mentor had him sand the floor and paint the fence, tasks that seemed unimportant to his goals.

My wish for you, with this book, is that you experience the Mr. Miyagi effect by having read this book. By that I mean that you've been posting regularly on social media, you've started a podcast, you're creating content and even though you don't see anything change soon, it'll bear fruit when you need it most. Paint the fence was a defense mechanism that protected Daniel-san, just like creating and putting out content will protect your business.

Some of what I teach here might be out of your comfort zone, thus uncomfortable, but by applying these things, you'll have the Mr. Miyagi effect. At the end of the day, you'll look back at difficult things you've gone through and say, "Wow, like putting socks on a rooster!" But you'll be happy, your employees will be happy, your business will be humming like a well-oiled machine, and most importantly, you'll have reached success as you've defined it to be for you.

Switzerland

I went to a conference a while ago and mingled with some people, which, by the way, is a necessary means of getting yourself and your business known. That conference resulted in a woman calling me six months later. When I picked up the phone, she told me she got my card from someone who met me at the conference. Our mutual acquaintance had told her, "When it comes to marketing, sales, and implementation, Mike is the guy to talk to," so she called me.

She had a partner and wanted to run their business model by me to get my opinion. As she told me about her business, I interjected with some clarifying questions. The way I saw it, they had a sound plan for their marketing and implementation but had no real direction on how to execute the sales portion. We talked more and I got to know her a little better, some of her likes, dislikes, hobbies, and how she likes to spend her time. She had told me about another project that had room for growth and that really excited her. It was apparent to me that the business she was in with her partner didn't excite her, but she thought it could be lucrative. At the end of the conversation, what I told her shocked her. I told her that I didn't think she had the passion for the company to do what it took to make the changes I felt the business needed. If she continued to work on that business with her partner, she would not have the bandwidth for the one that excited her. In essence, I closed the door on a potential client but it was the right thing to do. She thanked me and we went our separate ways.

About eight months later, I fielded a call from an odd number. It turned out, the lady calling me lived in Switzerland. She told me that the woman I had spoken to referred me to her. She had much success online but that the online world didn't resonate with her. Her mother was lying in what would be her deathbed and it changed the way the woman wanted to liver her life. "Kelly say's you're honest and know what you're talking about." I helped that woman from Switzerland transition to doing something that makes her life much more complete and satisfying.

I love working with people with a mission and a vision. My partner at Brand Ethos, Alicia Laszewski, and I are cautious of the prospects we convert to clients. Money should not be the only factor in deciding who to work with. There should also be a synergy that makes everything click and the relationship enjoyable. Such as it is with Lisa Collum. We've grown an amazing educational company and continue to expand it.

My experience has brought me on many stages and has allowed me to coach many business owners. Should you want to invite me to speak to your group or want to run your business processes by me, I'm more than willing to speak with you.

I leave you with this – always be honest and bring your core values into your business. This book, if you allow it, can help you find success, however you define it. But it's up to you to work on the implementation.

I can help.

ABOUT THE AUTHOR

Mike Ficara is a seasoned entrepreneur and consultant. His core focus is on the growth and scaling strategies for clients, in addition to expertise in personal brand building and social media strategy.

He has had the opportunity to work in a variety of industries over his career going from the classroom to the boardroom. This vast experience provided the insight into how people learn, leadership, and most importantly, what motivates people to succeed.

Through this, he has taken existing businesses and allowed them to see massive growth and stability through a variety of techniques and has consulted for small and large companies such as NEC, Nestle, Brand Ethos, and Top Score Writing, among others.

Given this knowledge and experience, today Mike spends his time coaching and consulting where he has the privilege of working with many successful business leaders as well as entrepreneurs.

Together, hard work and opportunity allowed them to grow several successful businesses in education, technology, healthcare, oil and gas, telecommunication, e-commerce, and manufacturing.

In addition, he has helped to consult on the development and training for creating a blended learning environment for several public, private, and charter schools across the United States.

Mike has worked with various enterprise clients to develop robust digital training programs along with strategic business plans to attack a variety of markets. Teamwork and self-motivation are something that are important to him and his team. He has a track record of bringing innovative ideas to clients and turning them into competitive products in their space.

Due to his wide range of experiences, he has been sought after to speak as an expert at several large conventions in a variety of industries across the United States and in International markets as well.

Mike is also the host of THE START DOWN PODCAST.

He currently possesses a BA in Psychology from Florida Atlantic University and a MS in Educational Media Design and Technology from Full Sail University. He is also involved in community and philanthropic ventures. During his free time, he enjoys spending time with his wife and their four children.

ACKNOWLEDGMENTS

To my children Michael, Anthony, Giovanni and Stella...you are the MAGS group! Thank you for always cheering Daddy on and being a part of my WHY!

To my Dad, thank you for teaching me all the great sayings, for example Like Socks on a Rooster. As a child, you exposed me to the world of entrepreneurship, and as an adult, you gave me a home to grow as an entrepreneur. I could not have done this without your guidance.

To my Mother, thank you for being by biggest fan. I appreciate you always cheering me on and supporting me on my journey.

To Natalia Diane, thank you so much for teaching me how to be Iron Man and not Robin! I could not think of anyone better to write the foreword to my book!

To Jim Eimmerman, thank you for opening the door to my educational career. Without you, I would have never gone down this road. You were a role model of faith and dedication from day one. Thank you for all you have done.

To Manny Riera, thank you for taking a chance on an extremely green entrepreneur and showing me the ropes, the canvas, the locker room and all the sides of business they never talk about!

To Lisa Collum, thank you for trusting me to be a part of your amazing journey in growing Top Score Writing. Your innovation and desire to help other people achieve success is something every child should learn in school!

To Alicia Laszewski, thank you for your friendship and partnership in business. Your never-ending desire to give 110% and serve is an amazing example of what all entrepreneurs should be.

To Vanessa Florido, for helping me be Jefe! A title I don't feel I always lived up to, but your support and dedication to the team is something I always appreciated.

To Ryan Griffiths, for being the backbone of everything we do as a company. Your willingness to grow and learn are key principles that will take you to the amazing places you desire to reach and beyond.

To Eli Gonzalez, thank you for all the effort you put into this book. You truly are the Godfather of Ghostwriting! You took my thoughts and put them into a story that I hope will help others achieve their dreams.

To my wife, Lauren, one more time. For all you do, a book dedication is not even enough to show my thanks. You are an amazing wife and mother. You teach me so much about leadership and sacrifice. I look forward to continuing this wild ride with you and seeing what else comes our way.

RECOMMENDED READING

The Columns: How to increase your lifestyle without increasing your income

By Frank Ficara

Cashflow & Grow: What it Takes to Build Your Business, Increase Your Revenue, and Pay Less at Tax Time.

By Tyler McBroom

You Need More Money: Wake Up and Solve Your Financial Problems Once And For All

By Matt Manero

You, Inc Discover the CEO Within

By Burke Hedges

Don't Let Your Struggle Become Your Standard: How to Be Indispensable Even When the Odds Are Stacked Against You

By Jose Flores

CPSIA information can be obtained
at www.ICGtesting.com
Printed in the USA
JSHW031324030223
37197JS00001B/6

9 781737 153191